Scars for Future Wars

JORDAN JONGEMA

Contents

CHAPTER 1

A Memory Best Served Cold

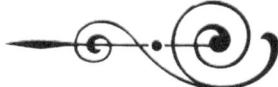

The following collection of events contains zero fabrications. During these journaled adventures, a multitude of characters weaved their way into and out of my moral code of existence. Many are buried, but many still live. The only alteration of reality was a few words of dialogue exchanged between myself and others, plus the name of one ex-girlfriend, due to the request for her privacy. I tried my best to remember each and every precise detail with blooming reactivity. I've indicated via dates and locations where I was in the world for each wave of belligerent beatdowns my body put up with. Some chapters are in chronological order, while others flip the pages of the calendar back and forth a few years.

There was only so much my mind and soul could handle until I almost departed to the dirt during a fateful bender in the apocalyptic Winter of January 2023. While nearly all of these experiences would have forced my Family to bring forth a Gravestone for me far too early, the previously mentioned upheaval of insanity that happened in 2023 was the harshest form of Alcohol Withdrawal a human being is forced to undergo, leading to an internal cataclysmic transcendence to other realms, balancing on a poorly made teeter-totter weighed down on the side of death.

I do my best to bring you directly to where I have gone (and thankfully returned from).

While there were unchartable amounts of joyous times I've had with alcohol on the night's menu, allowing me to strip myself of an introverted shell acquired for most of my time spent awake, bringing me closer to the bonds shared with family & friends, playing in bands and performing live music for over fifteen years, travelling the globe, and it being the reason why I met some of the most important people in my life to this day; this is a weak excuse to try and ignore the immeasurable amount of damage it began to exhibit nearing the final days of drinking.

It has been agonizing to relive the Alcoholic Warfield and PTSD-soaked memories of the past, but I felt it was necessary as an integral part of the process of healing. A revolting relapse was definitely breathing down my neck during the course of composing all of this. However, there is nothing more cathartic than analyzing your demons on paper, attentively working with them, understanding each angle to its puzzle, eventually coming to a mutual agreement, and shaking hands with them. More individuals need to find the amount of eventual relief from engaging in this activity. It is by no means a cakewalk or a joyous road of bright Sun and pleasant aromatic Forests. It is more like navigating through a moonlit dirt road with a flickering mini-flashlight, avoiding traps set by psychotic mountain hermits, and trying not to be mauled by fanged ghouls. Convert the notion of Fear into a partner you wish to walk with for the rest of your life. Let it hold your blood-caked hands as the both of you travel inside a hurricane of hollowpoint bullets. If it has the capacity to stop your life in its tracks, why would it not have the potential to help thrust you forward?

Inhale.

Listen to where it's guiding you.

Exhale.

This is the reality of when Alcoholism has found a way to ravage ruthlessly inside your soul, offering the chance to murder you every morning and night but also trying to caress you to the rhythmic waves of a comfortable heartbeat, to love you unconditionally at the same time.

The rewarding agony of discipline will correct the faults found in your spine.

- Jordan Jongema
January 2025 Penticton, B.C., Canada

CHAPTER 2

Drinking from the Ozone Layer

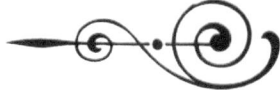

__July 2017__
__Abbotsford, B.C., Canada__

I'm standing outside my Apartment building, wrapped feverishly amongst the weather relative to a Vulture-infested Desert. It's around 36°C, and the humidity is like collecting a bucket of saliva from each individual at your local dive bar and pouring it over your face. My brain feels like I've got an aneurysm incoming. The power & strength of Gravity has been increased with each wobbly step. My hair looks like the Greek God Zeus did a quick rail of street-grade Cocaine and cast a Tornado directly into my head. What else is wrong with me? Have I been transferred to the planet of Mercury? My blood pressure is almost caustic. Every time I blink my eyes, some sizzling spark embarks on a tap dancing exhibition up & down my insides. I am a baitless hook in a fishless pond. With the roof of the sky appearing to cave in on me, I wish all of these feelings of the morning would fade into the wisps of spilt milk cloud trails above.

Here's to lessening the worry. I take a swig of Alcohol.

My Realtor is beside me with an array of flashy documents. While hastily scribbling my initials with my right hand, a can of Mike's Hard Lemonade in the other, I'm about to sign the official Bill of Sale for the Apartment I purchased last year. The grip on my drink far outweighs the accuracy of the pen.

I signed the wrong area. This was in permanent ink—as permanent as the looming hangovers that stuck a scythe in my spinal cord for years gone by and for years to come. Embarrassed and fighting off the withdrawal shakes, I told my Realtor maybe he should reprint another document and come back in an hour. While saying this, I pulled another Cooler out of my back pocket and offered it to him. He checked his watch and laughed.

"No, no. I'm good," he insisted, "It's too early, man. We'll cross this out, and you can sign down here."

He had been filming this sale for his Instagram account, and all was caught with his camera—more lush evidence of my idiocy.

I suggested he return in an hour so I could stumble back upstairs to shotgun a few Coolers. He said he'd figure it out once he returned to his office. After this process, I could bolt through & conquer (with such an inflated ego & cockiness) a marathon of staggering proportions. It turns out it would just be a Marathon of Staggering—nothing is impressive about it. Just the Alcohol flashing & beaming at me with productivity.

While I had shared a few inebriated and liquor-ridden nights with my Realtor in the past, I never got the chance to know him personally. I remember him as sharp and punctual, so when given the opportunity to have him on board to sell my apartment, I lunged towards the notion of briefly inviting him on my sinking ship of alcoholic delights. However, the magic that more considerable sums of Money can do to the bonding experience of two people is quite fascinating on the Materialistic front. Does each fake word exchange add another dollar to the bank? I'm not too fond of it. It feels incredibly wishy-washy and *let's just pretend we're friends so we can get paid, and maybe we'll bump into each other in the future.* I could see the Dollar Bills glowing in his pupils and glimmering in mine.

Trying to wipe the sweat from my shaking hands, I extend my palm to meet my Realtor. He chimes in on wanting to wine & dine me tonight due to the big sale we just closed off. I respond with a "FUCK YEAH!" but in reality, a slow-dripping IV bag of poison is coating the insides of my Skull, realizing this will be another night evolving into a panic-stricken sunrise due to the waterfall of booze to be consumed.

We both were ecstatic to bundle this process up and bootfuck it off a cliff. However, I felt this cliff was placed in the core of an overflowing city for thousands to watch me dive after it, plummeting facefirst to the graven concrete. Of course, I'd pour a drink in my mouth on the descent downward.

After the whole paper signing exchange, I watched him leave in his *what every Realtor in existence would own* vehicle. I guzzled down the rest of my Hard Lemonade and stared up at the sky.

There's something about the viciousness of the morning Sun entering your body as you struggle to not pass out from Alcohol Withdrawal. With a nail-covered backhand, it reminds you of the sweet, blistering definition of dehydration. It qualifies you a singeing gold medal across your collarbone, handed by a freakish overlord of the underground in the Olympics of Hell, slowly burning through your chest cavity and playing hopscotch with your organs.

Heading back into my residence, I opened the second Cooler I was going to cheer with my Realtor. I commence in *slamming* it, feeling very pleased that he declined to drink it. I crave this so severely that I could almost eat the entire can. The aroma of chemical-ridden Lemonade. The sweet and moving elixir that both slaughters and heals.

During this, I pass by a Woman in the Elevator who looks down at the drink in my hand. It's probably 10:00 am, and we're both analyzing the Alcohol in our presence this early. She's wondering why I'm drinking at this hour. I'm wondering why I don't have two or three more in my pocket (and you're damn right if you think I've tried to fit more than four in my Jeans before, the shape of the cans protruding out, looking as ridiculous as possible). Politely nodding, I then make a juvenile attempt to hide the container behind my back.

The Elevator is slow (I'm only on the fourth floor), but I can ever so slightly feel those two drinks I've already had (in quick succession) start to work their beauty.

I make it to my room and place the two empties on the counter. I'm not one of those Neanderthals who crush their can

& toss it irresponsibly when they're done with it. I allow every last drop of purified nectar to be appropriately managed down my throat before retiring the aluminum to the recycling bin. You can throw down the endless scroll of how many ways I've become a reject, but at least I still retain a pebble's worth of decency.. at least in the eyes of the Environmentalists.

In an action that has become all too familiar throughout my life, I place my head in my hands for a brief moment. My fingers are spread open to see what's in front of me, but my hands remain across my face.

I've just sold my apartment, which I've only owned for a year and a half, with no backup plan or guidelines for the future. All of this was done on a youthful, inebriated whim of cash it in now or be a slave for 20+ years.

Since I started to put $75 to $100 of every paycheque into a savings account for the last five years (with my work matching it with their contribution), I was able to buy a piece of real estate at 24 years old. Millennials often bitch & whine about not being able to afford a place of their own, but if you pull up your big boy or girl pants and implement a financial plan in your late teens, diligently sticking to it, you will be able to afford something by the time you are in your mid 20's.

While I stayed employed and climbed the ranks quickly at my job of seven and a half years in the Heavy Duty Trucking industry, my hangovers were becoming more apparent, eventually keeping me from exiting my bedroom. A few months prior, I quit my job to not have to deal with the repercussions of my attendance and declining performance. Though I was half the age of everyone else who worked in my department, I held seniority. I was given far too many chances to make changes. They relied on me to make it to work and help run the show. I did us both a favour.

I look down and see my old tattoos. The two engravings I have on each forearm of *Inhale/Exhale* coexist with the philosophy of Meditation, often reminding me to keep the innate tools as active as ever in such situations as these. An oceanic trench of a deep breath occurs, and I move my hands across my head, lightly pulling my hair back.

My eyes lock on the fridge. There's more alcohol in there.

A few months prior, my ex-girlfriend, Emily, hit the road and got the hell out of this alcoholic armageddon-stirring apartment. I still have a photographic image/memory that replays of her standing in my Kitchen/Living Room, her belongings in boxes scattered together, with a look of defeat & heartbreak on her face (I will become accustomed to this look by almost every girlfriend I've ever had). In this Memory, I was quickly returning home from the Bar to grab something after I had told her I'd make a better commitment to quit drinking. My friend is waiting downstairs for me in his truck. Here I am, stumbling back through the front door. She's putting together her travel bags and formulating her exit plan.

"I just wish you'd quit drinking.. forever," she softly mumbles with a complete, open faucet of tears in her eyes.

I'm at the point of a perfect buzz where my focus isn't quite the tough chief in command. I stare at the ground and bite my bottom lip. I have no clue what to tell her.

She's put up with this for almost eight months. The first few months were somewhat tolerable; she could tag along with me wherever I went, probably thinking this wouldn't be permanent.

Never was I ever abusive to her, but I could have projected myself with finer quality. I recall the first few months with content & well-being. The final few were listless and aimless in being a worthwhile boyfriend/partner. It's not appealing.

Her ecstatic pleas of wanting to explore British Columbia and other parts of the world were always cut short by my increasingly pummelling hangovers. The avalanches of my self-promises smothered our snowboarding and skiing expeditions to obliteration and blackout spells.

I had managed to quit drinking for a few weeks at a time, but as soon as the ominous & seductive howls from the forbidden jungles pouring with Alcohol called my name, I answered back as loudly as humanly possible. I don't blame her for bouncing out. However, I let her move in with me far too early - another element of my psyche that is lopsided too far into the trait of agreeableness. This is second-degree murder in a relationship.

The returning memory has found its way out the door. I open the fridge, grab a sizzling cold Hard Lemonade, and hold it up in the air, the way Rafiki from The Lion King embraces Simba to the Animals below. Unbeknownst to me - the potion of life & death rests chillingly in my palms. I sign a five-year pact with it down a trail of landmines in the guise of gemstones, a romantic deal with Earthbound Angels fluttering around with meathooks for wings, and one of the biggest fallacies known to Humanity that the contents in these cans/bottles will bring a responsible unity between fellow counterparts and myself.

The promise of a night lathered in character transformation through liquid courage is kept, and my Realtor gets me downright gooned after the Sale of my previously owned Apartment goes through. This lands me close to $245,000. I have to pay off the remainder of my Mortgage and give him his chunk of fleshy green bills, but I'm still walking away with +$55,000. A definite danger to be boiling in the bank account of a young adult clinging to an electric fence in an ocean of hedonism and turmoil.

We bar-hop around town. The sauce is poured and consumed as if we've finally accepted that the End Times will impale us with centuries of expectation. I ended up meeting one of my best friends, Mitchell, during all of this. One of my brothers in all that is havoc-ridden disruption, Mitch and I have been turning the distortion & master volume knobs to *11* since we met during Guitar class in 2007. He was in Grade 9, myself in Grade 11. We were first introduced to each other one morning when I was assigned to teach him a few patterns of guitar theory. During this class, I brought a Coke bottle half full of Jack Daniels that I was planning to drink all day at school. I gave him a whiff of the open container; instead of being appalled, he laughed his ass off and asked for a sip. Right then and there, we established a deep-rooted connection based on metal music, guitars, and booze. Comically enough, throughout that school year, I'd drop off canned Rockstar Vodka drinks at his locker if I had any left over from the weekend. Our skills in hallway espionage were flawless. That or the school was just too focused on their elite students to bother caring what anyone else did. I knew right away we'd be best buddies for life. For the next ten years, we'll go as hard as humanly possible in the art of nuclear-partying-warfare. With fury like the hammer of an otherworldly God crashing down onto a battle cruiser-sized anvil, we formed multiple bands together, playing handfuls of shows downtown Vancouver, being lit to kingdom come for most of its entirety, and somehow were able to walk away (somewhat) unscathed and without a criminal record (for now). The predicaments and heights we climb (and fall) are unforgettable. I'd trade some of my most prized instruments to try it over again (with hopes of less cauterizing outcomes).

Other accomplices tag along on this extravagant night of stretching the bar tab around the planet as many times as possible, knowing as soon as we let go of it, it'll whip back and decimate our bank accounts. In some sort of sick ranking system, when we are done sucking from the taps of one bar, we migrate to another. There's no definitive reasoning behind doing this. Does the quality of beer, wine, or spirits matter when you're far past your limit and ready to project it all back into the toilet? All of these nights come with the possibility of adding a DUI to the list of ill-ridden badges to wear with alcoholic honour.

The hours churn about and rise to the void above, never to be seen again. I wake up in the early morning hours on the bathroom floor, back in my empty apartment. There's a pillow beside the toilet. The shower is running. This becomes my routine and area of comfort when I'm feeling nauseous or past the point of nearly suffocating on my night's choices. Aside from the divine anxiolytic massage of Benzodiazepines, the ASMR-style drizzle of the shower is one of the only things that can provide me with a blanketing calm while undergoing withdrawal in the morning.

In these early days, I never scientifically understood how *hair of the dog* in the morning can alleviate nearly 99.9% of the symptoms of Alcohol Withdrawal. I had just figured out this equation of "alcohol in the morning = a day free of panic" the previous week when I had a Tinder date, Kelsey, stay the night with me. I had to wipe my mouth clean of drool after first matching with her, gawking over her angelic features, her perfect height of 5'3, a combination of Emo chimes with hardcore flowing black hair, and that kind of curious and playful personality found in animals who have just been released from their cage (perhaps a warning I ignored). Our first meeting was at a small diner in the city of Chilliwack, where we immediately trauma-bonded over our past & current lives. Something about Kelsey, perhaps the devilish appeal of her aesthetic and seductive smile or her frisky giddiness, drew me closer to walking in the middle of a busy freeway. Our first night out together was a sloppy alcoholic massacre, committing harakiri to our brains via endless shots of Jagerbombs and citrus ciders. By the end of the night, she wandered off with two randoms, and I found her making out with them outside in an alleyway. After spending the last few weeks getting closer to this girl, I felt gouged in the back with a drill the size of a telephone pole. I left her at the bar and walked home, smashing a few things on the way back.

When I returned to my apartment, I forgot she had left her dog at my place. I knew she would have to return to get him, so I spent an hour drunkenly talking to him while lying on the ground.

She eventually stumbled back to my residence, where I let her in, tried to ignore what had previously happened, and we spent the night drinking more vodka, eventually passing out in bed together. The following morning, whether it was to deal with the awkwardness of waking up beside this dark-haired princess who breathed fire or to manage the withdrawals, I immediately grabbed the ¾ full bottle of Absolut Vodka off my dresser drawer and began to drink like a parched athlete would after a rigorous race. I drove her home later that morning, still with the bottle in my hand. She'd go to play around with me for another month. The first night should have been a red flag to cease all operations, but the temptation was unbearable. The last time I saw her, she came over, seduced me, and right before it was about to happen, got up, put her clothes back on, and walked out of my apartment. From here on out, I refer to her as "Queen Blue Balls".

This morning, I considered doing my body a favour by not drinking and trying to fight off this anxious, irritable and mentally fissuring breakdown on my own. It was wishful thinking. The bottle screams my name through a megaphone jammed directly into my auditory canals. Just enough frequency to make me entirely deaf, except for when adhering to its words of dominating force, listening only to it.

I started to get *the shakes* at just 25 years old. I don't know if this is what having untreated Parkinson's Disease feels like, but it's often unmanageable without chemical interference.

It's taken a horrendously heavy amount of alcohol abuse to reach the signs of withdrawal at a younger age. I genuinely believe the physiology of the human body remains in tatters if you don't give your brain enough time to repair in the mornings of a binging episode; the damage only evolves from there. Those who drink in the early hours of the day to ease withdrawal symptoms play a deadly game of cat and mouse. I guess I was just too goddamn stubborn to want to have to put up with the unsettling cacophony of hangovers. The first few times I began to have more moderate withdrawal symptoms landed me in the hospital due to waves of panic that came with it: Heart palpitations, slippery palms, syncope, severe derealization, and a feeling of complete emotional insanity.

I had no clue about what *withdrawal* was. We were never warned in elementary or high school about these dreaded outcomes. We were continually force-fed the fear of drug use reigning "Kings & Queens of the Bad Guys" to be hanging around with, never the booze. I wish to wipe the floor clean of these morons who fail to implement a more robust warning system for younger generations.

The fact that Alcohol holds such world-shattering power and is given the green light by all forms of authority makes it much more dangerous than anything else in the existence of Humanity. Period.

Imagine a substance readily available from 9 am to 11 pm (even later at Pubs/nightclubs) that fixates a high percentage of the world's population on extreme violence, sexual depravity, crime-ridden fantasies that evolve into reality, layers of mental & physical health complications, butchering all of your life's work in the foreground & background in just one single bottle… and this is the one that's legal and publicized on commercial after commercial to keep your business/social life top-notch, having you submit to it along with every other poor son of a bitch being fondled by its predatory hand.

I visited my Doctor after each hospital visit and tried to obtain a grasp on what was happening to me. I was given a Holter monitor to wear to document my heart palpitations, prescribed anti-depressants (which, mixed with alcohol, gave me blinding blackouts until, after a few months, I flushed down the toilet and never retook them), and was told to learn to manage my stress better.

A few nights mixing the anti-depressant Escitalopram with a night of binging had me leaving the bar in a blackout, walking home while the rest of my friends were still at the bar, confused as to where the hell I wandered off to. Many times, I'd manage to make it back to my bedroom (sometimes walking across town) in a completely unconscious state and wake up the next morning fully clothed, still wearing my shoes, face down in bed.

I even admitted to my Doctor that I loved to drink, and it got out of hand mostly every time I would do so. His only words were, "Just try to manage what you can."

The severity of my addiction was not addressed but instead ignored (it is not until seven years later a different doctor will tell me there is no scientific research that's ever been successful for using anti-depressants to help with alcohol addiction).

Each insane overhaul of a bender would leave me shuddering, like being left to freeze outside of a barracks at the north tip of Finland in the middle of a December snowstorm. This feeling was absolutely god awful, and until I figured out how to curb it with more alcohol, the suffering was unimaginable. No deep breathing or meditative yoga courses could pull me from the on-edge near state of delirium I'd undergo after drinking heavily for days into weeks.

As I pull myself off the bathroom floor and survey the emptiness of the Apartment that no longer belongs to me, I'm nearly incapacitated with the feeling of an invisible Anaconda twisting around my body, squeezing with each movement I make toward my Kitchen. What feels like death throes throws me into my Kitchen table, stumbling upon a bottle of leftover Vodka. I rip it off the table. These first few gulps are swallowed with pinpoint accuracy, being consumed at an alarming rate to murder the creature of the jungle being welded to my skin. I hold my breath, fighting back tears, feeling like my entire body is going to seize up.

The wave of magnificence arrives and places me back onto a gelatin, serene cloud of inner peace & quietude. I let the alcohol take its course. To the bottle - What transforms Men into Monsters, what aids as the reason for one's failures, what will place a steel-toed boot on the back of your head as you lay helplessly facedown in a puddle of your own vomit and drowns you in front of your family - here it is, folks.

It might be the sunlight breathing through my blinds or the overall feelings of a Summer in decline; I'm reminded of a shadow-ridden time when I was 19 years old and experiencing equal amounts of mental corruption.

CHAPTER 3

Creekside Colours

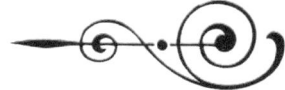

Early June 2011
Yarrow, B.C., Canada

Peeling my face off of a park bench in the glazen froth of midday June, I'm regaining consciousness from an intoxicated, perilous adventure - a morning & day drinking combination that fails to make sense to me. My shoes & shirt seemed to have vanished. There are hundreds of people within voice range all around. The humming of life throws me another dumbbell to blindly catch in a cloud of unease and brings forth thoughts gaping with cavities. I'm slumped over on a bench at the Skatepark in the small country town of Yarrow. Butterflies skim off my shoulder blades. Muttered voices sizzle across the park like a small city coming to life after a period of dismal silence. Today is the yearly event/party the townsfolk call "Yarrow Days". You'd think someone might have noticed a boy in his teens out cold on a park bench and alerted authorities. This would/could/should have saved me from the unfolding of distress, both physically and mentally. All of this is wishful thinking.

Earlier, I was rummaging about the riversides and levees with one of my ex-girlfriends, Danielle, and her new troupe of friends. Danielle & I had been on and off for the last few months. I could feel how annoyed she was to have me around, but she never summoned the courage to say it outright. Being 19 years of age didn't provide me with the favourable knowledge to be my own Superhero and save myself from the ravenous incoming firestorm. Being around her today was freakish, and I felt like my head was stuck in an echo chamber, the sounds of regret returning with continuous, pummelling fists.

My current state of almost being naked in public and without a clue in the world about what was happening confirms that I most likely made a complete ass of myself in front of her & the rest of the watching eyes. I remember being in a random person's house, off a country road, slamming back whisky as if my life depended on it. I lost every person I was partying with in a haze of delusion and coma-like suppression of my motor functions. I drank 750ml of Alberta Premium Whisky in less than four or five hours. Flashes of strangers appear in my now-awakened mind. I remember bumping into a group of girls and being so intoxicated that I started to speak half-gibberish and half-Russian to them (I had taken a University course in Russian nine months before this; it still is somewhat fresh in the Wernicke's Area of my brain). Out of all these flashbacks, what upsets me the most was being left behind by Dani and the others whom I was partying with. A straggler sent to the dirt and forgotten like napkins raped after a Smorgasbord. Still, things aren't making much sense.

A few minutes pass. I smack the pockets around my legs to search for my keys. With much chaotic success, they are still in my right pocket. I feel for my phone & wallet. Both of those are in the corresponding left & back pockets. Every time I make physical contact with my BlackBerry phone, I'm reminded of my unstable hatred towards the device. However, if I had to walk away from this day with the success of keeping all three of those, it would have been a grandiose and well-fought battle. Things did not shape out that way.

The silhouette of my car is about 500 metres from where I passed out/am still sitting. I figure I can shift into Pink Panther mode and slyly sneak over to my vehicle without giving too much of myself away. As drunk as I am, my legs don't resemble jelly as I stand up and straighten myself out. I make the march to the driver's seat. I pass by a police officer on the way over. We don't make eye contact. I believe he's gone on his way, focusing on other matters at this human-flooded event. As I enter my car, I see him leave towards the busy park. I let out one of the largest sighs of relief, probably near-melting the inside fabric of my car from my breath replete with alcohol, and put the key into the ignition. From here, there is a disorienting plume of lunacy that throws my memory into a vibrating pool inside of a Black Hole. Time deletes itself. A paradox of inactivity and causation elope. Loud music swims through my auditory canals and brings vision back to my eyes. Suddenly, there is a bright, emerald-green view of a Willow

Tree quickly making its way toward me, or I am making my projection toward it. No swerving. The sound is like nothing I've ever heard before. I don't have time to analyze or chew on it. The only thing I'm about to eat is my Windshield as I fly into it.

There's a small trickling of ditch water seeping around my feet. No more music. Leaves. Strands of grass. Small bugs. Shards of glass. Blood. A rotten and extremely pungent stench of an unknown powder nearly knocks me out cold again. While the front half of my body was being sent under the rearview mirror of the car, the impact of the airbag threw me towards the passenger seat. I wasn't wearing my seatbelt. I became a human pinata performing for the neck-breaking laws of physics. I stare out the windshield for a few minutes, which looks like spider webs lit up with a flamethrower. I look down and see my pelvis and hands are cut up. It's nothing severe, but there's blood all over the airbag. That unknown powder scent is coming from the airbag being deployed. Few things obtain such an unappetizing aroma. Not only is one left to try and maintain their physical injuries after an airbag is deployed, but that smell lingers around like a Hyena taunting you after you've undergone a traumatic event. Just the extra *fuck you* to have to flick you in the ear with everything it's got.

I try opening my driver's door to no avail. It's wedged into the sand deposits in the ditch I've plummeted down into. With no recollection of doing so, I had both of my windows open before I crashed. I use this to my advantage and drunkenly pull myself through the opening of the driver-side window. Three realizations pierce through me. I'm lucky not to have crashed right into the Willow Tree, perhaps hitting the brakes in some apparent stimulation still hanging on in my visual cortex. I'm also severely lucky for the month of June, which makes these Ditches reasonably empty of water. Had this been other months, I would have drowned a nasty death in high waters filled with animal feces and festering bacteria. The third thought was: Did I break the full Heineken bottles in my trunk? I could use one of those right now.

I climb across the car's hood, over the sunroof, and roll down across the trunk, landing in the tall grass at the edges of the ditch. I use my key to try to open my trunk. It thankfully opens. The heavy lid is propelled upward, and I'm shown the treasures from the deep. The sight of unbroken Heineken bottles curls my broken smile towards the sky. Grabbing the bottle and observing its glisten in the Sun is like plunging your hands into a liquid disco ball and experiencing the reflections of light spin your soul into resuscitation and born-again brilliance. There's an odd gust of sedating assurance lurking about as a multitude of birds fly by, chirping and turning around the Willow Trees surrounding me. Maybe they're laughing at my stupidity. Perhaps they're sending their regards to the loser below.

I begin to call dozens, if not hundreds, of people on my phone, forgetting 99% of anything I say to them. I figure the best time to catch up on conversations with people is when I've almost killed myself and am sitting in a jumbled mess of vehicular suicide. For some reason, I dial my ex-girlfriend's best friend. I have no idea why, but I call her close to ten times. I called the people I was with a few hours earlier. None of them answered. I'm most likely being ignored as I'm in one of my belligerent drunken states, one which is hard to be around. I get ahold of two of my best friends. They're currently watching game two of the Stanley Cup Final Hockey game at home. They're both drinking, not nearly as drunk as I am. Both of them have no clue what to say other than, "Get the fuck out of there and go home!" I figured this would be a good idea. I'm hesitant, but I will make one more call to my parents, who are barely just four kilometres from where I crashed. I know they're currently holding a house party. My Mom answers. The concern in her voice stays with me for a while. There must be an innate defensive mechanism that is engulfed with a neurological response when you hear a caring parent with worry in their voice. While I am only a three-minute drive from their house, they don't make an effort to try and help me out. I'm a little pissed off, but I start to realize I'm about to turn 20 in a few months, and these are the types of things I'll have to figure out for myself.

There's a possibility I have a concussion due to sending myself 70/80kmh into the ditch to Zero in a split second. I take a moment to drink one of the Heinikens, foolishly thinking this could further the betterment of my situation, and ponder my current framework down to every last bent nail. For a moment, it feels great. After finishing one of the green bottles of glory, I climb to the top of the ditch beside the road. A few people drive by, craning their necks as if they could spin their vertebrae freely like the child from The Exorcist. Some keep proceeding, but others stop and ask if I'm doing okay. Here is a shirtless and shoeless kid looking visibly out of his mind, telling them to "keep on going and to have a nice day." Two younger adults stop their truck and look the most concerned out of the folks who've already assessed my situation. Once again, I'm so mentally polluted with surviving the force of the car crash & already dehydrated, beat up, deprived of daily nutrients and have had my go through the grater. Still, I switch from speaking English to Russian, weaving in and out of incoherent ramblings of a swelling brain pumping with booze and adrenaline. Both men appear to have had a few drinks, too. They laugh the situation away. I tell them to get the hell out of here, and I'll take care of it myself.

My first & last order of business is to try and summon a Tow Truck to help get this collection of metal & flat tires out of the ditch and over to my Parent's house. A few companies I've dealt with at work appear in my list of options. I got a hold of a Towing Company located in Abbotsford, roughly 30 minutes away. My choice of diction and tone in my voice is a dead giveaway of being granted my PhD as Professor Plastered. I barely remember my phone conversation with the company. After a few minutes of vocal struggle, I'm able to provide them with the coordinates for where my car has taken refuge from the roads above. I hang the phone up and spit out micro elements of glass. It lands on the ends of a Cattail weed. I've visibly tattooed Mother Nature with a millilitre of my blood. I sit beside it and wish to be cleansed by the ether in the sky for all this wrongdoing.

I haven't the slightest clue how to explain this to my parents, but I know once I get there, I can hide in my room and pass out until the day fades into the next.

The familiar groaning of a large Tow Truck spawns in the distance. I get up to my feet and squint my eyes towards where I hear the sounds. Approaching me is a large Truck, attached with the necessary equipment to drag cars in any direction. Behind it are two Police cruisers. The dispatch employee I spoke with on the phone alerted the Police, with utmost certainty, of how wasted I was. I'm left to mouth only one sole expletive.

The cops are swift and rude. I did not expect the Boys in Blue to accompany the Tow Truck on its rescue mission. I've had no time to work an alibi into a presentable piece of art. All I have to show for is my pants around my ankles and my dick in my hands.

One of the officers asked if I was the one driving. I spit out a ridiculous flub and say that one of my friends was with me, but he took off on foot. They aren't purchasing any of my bullshit stocks on this embarrassing day on the stock market.

"If we test the blood on the airbag and it comes back as your DNA, you are in severe trouble," the cop yells in frustration.

As a young kid, I'm entirely cornered from all directions of the compass. I have no clue what to do but drop to my knees in defeat and tell the truth. I'm administered a Breathalyzer twice and fail miserably each time. I was hoping the machine would glitch out, catch fire, and turn everything a blaze within 100 feet of me - that's when I'd head south, screaming and running like the Tasmanian Devil if he just injected four cans of Redbull into his arm. It doesn't happen. I'm placed in the back of the cop car. As I watch through the back window, the Tow Truck hauls my destroyed vehicle out of the ditch. The front end of it compressed in like an accordion of steel. I imagine what note my Car would make as if it were an accordion being played on the street. I notice one of the officers picking up one of the Heiniken bottles. He shakes his head and laughs.

None of this seems to phase me. I'm still drunk enough to not give a single fuck (perhaps, also concussed). Being in the back of a cop car makes me laugh inside as I imagine having to spend the rest of the night in jail. Popping my cherry on saying I've been behind bars and had the glory of sleeping on a concrete slab, pissing into a metallic toilet where the sink rests on its top, and the bodily fluids & stench of previous attendees are still caked into the grime on the floor. What a pure and glorious joy.

Both of the police officers get back into the car. I asked them about the NHL Stanley Cup final that's currently in progress. Even with the incoming suspension of my driver's license, destroying my car, and having to embrace a wave of financial depression to deal with all this - all I cared about was Hockey. The Vancouver Canucks are facing the Boston Bruins in game two of seven. I can't remember what they told me. In an attempt to save what dignity I have left, I ask the Officers if they are able to bring me home. I live 3km from this crash site, and even though it felt badass at the time, it would make no sense for them to haul me to the drunk tank or a jail cell. While the laws of drinking and driving were still stiff in 2011, the Cops reluctantly agreed to bring me back home. Perhaps they took a good glance at how dreadful my current existence was and were able to bleed some sympathy for a shirtless punk who had just survived a toe-to-toe match with death.

We drive for a mere three minutes. The fields of Yarrow look like a candle that's been lit for too long, running out of wax but still retaining its amber glow. I feel the vial of my youth being emptied. The rear seats of a cop car could very well be the most uncomfortable mouldings of plastic ever to be produced. This uneven stone-hard block I'm sitting on reminds me of those trays used to take away dishes in a restaurant. Did they melt all of these together in one gigantic vat and form them into these thick bricks of grey?

In one final attempt to keep myself from further embarrassment, I ask the badged duo if I can be dropped off a few hundred metres from my house. I told them my parents were having a house party, and it would be alarming to every soul there to see the Son of the party holders show up, bruised & shirtless, escorted by Police Officers. Again, they agree. I smirk a little and am grateful these two guys are relatively easy-going. Maybe they were shit disturbers back in their day and could relate, or perhaps they had their lives together, felt terrible, and were never faced with plunging their faces into a ten-year skirmish with barbaric Alcoholism like I was.

The Police drop me off a hundred yards south of the large Willow Tree that protects my parent's front yard. I stuff the ticket the Cops have written me into the back of my jeans pocket. I thank the two men in Uniforms for dropping me back off home and for being tolerable - whatever the fuck that means. They take off northbound, down the road. The arid countryside boils around my skin like warming plates of animal fat on top of a rustic stove. I begin the walk. There's little left of my energy levels. I look up and notice over seven or eight cars in my parent's driveway. I've made it home after facing a gruelling day of debauchery and stopping a quarterway through digging my grave. I go through the garage and walk into the Kitchen, where there are too many people for me to handle. My parents found me and asked what had happened. I'm trying my best to keep it together and not be too vocal about what had just happened, as one of the families who are at this party lost their Son to a car accident just a few years prior. He had been doing the same thing as I just did. In mid-2007, he left a party in the early morning hours and crashed directly into a thick & fortified tree. Perhaps he passed out and never saw it coming. From what I remember, they calculated he was travelling over 120kmh before impact. His crash site was about 10km from mine. His death was a shock to my entire family, especially myself, as we were one year apart in age.

I grew up with him throughout my elementary school years. We went to the same high school together but separated as we found different groups of friends. As young kids, we used to *dig to China* in sandboxes, watch wrestling, game it up on Nintendo 64, and play floor hockey for years. He was the first person I knew closely to have passed away. Going to his open casket was a life changer. Walking into that room and seeing him propped in the casket, an organ-less collection of dead skin was not settling at all. As my Dad followed behind me into the viewing room, he immediately turned a blinding sheet of pale white, almost passing out from the sight. There are specific images in life that will never take flight away from you.

I tell my parents that it's all taken care of, and I'll have to figure out how to get my car out of the impound once it's allowed to leave after it's held hostage for 30 days. This isn't the sort of situation you want to have in the middle of a party you're trying to host. I recognize this and retreat to my room.

I'm left to lay on my bed and gaze at the indents in the ceiling. I've been contacting a few people on my phone this whole time. I still haven't heard back from anyone I was with earlier in the day. Receiving the cold shoulder from Danielle all day gives me a few more hours to host my own pity party. This deeply enraged me.

I texted a few friends that we should meet up. I don't want to be here, so I leave the house, walking down the road towards Abbotsford. This would be a 20km walk; therefore, the looming haze of the sun would transpire to darkness when I arrived in the city. I make it about ten minutes before I hear my Dad driving up the road towards me. He says I need to calm down and take a breather. We go back to the house. Most of my parent's friends are cautiously side-eyeing me as if they have heard what is happening. The hockey game is on the big screen in the living room, the music is loud, and the sun is still out - I ignore all ounces of negativity. This is the foundation of dealing with traumatic events in this household: the use of Alcohol to mask the weight of fundamental truths, failure ever to be reprimanded for one's faults, and the dawning of a mask of normality to outside eyes that everything is okay.

I bullshit my Dad that I'll drink a beer with him and his buddies, and then I'm going to go to bed, as the day has been one of the heaviest boatloads of chaos I've had to deal with ever in my life. We drank and watched a bit more of the hockey game. The game is tied 2-2 and headed to overtime. Going to bed when the game's stakes are that intense should have been an indicator to anybody of sound mind, but nobody questions it. I retire to my room and close the door.

One of my best friends, Chase, would like to meet up with me to confirm that I'm not dead. A high school bestie, Chase, and I were a musical match made in heaven the moment we turned power chords into brotherhood. Consider us the Simon & Garfunkle of Grindcore. A few years back, during our final high school & post-high school times, both of us committed all of our efforts outside of our assigned classrooms to the band we formed one staggeringly hungover morning in 2008. As 16 & 17-year-olds, we were able to play underage at a few bars in Vancouver and begin to stoke the embers of the underground grind/metal scene as toddlers behind our instruments (which helped land us future gigs as we aged). If Chase invented a guitar riff, I'd help finish it with some maniacal drums, our fluid chemistry proving to be as reactionary as a chain of starter fluid linking with any flame protruding device. Though we raised hell and marched around in public with beer boxes over our heads, Chase seemed to be a little more grounded than most of my other friends (perhaps having a more secure & less turbulent family life).

We play a brief game of Pong in the form of text messages.

Now that my car's front end has been crushed inwards and its components drained of necessary & required fluids, I agree to walk and meet him, even though it's going to take almost four hours to get into town. I wasn't expecting to get picked up, as virtually every single person I know is drinking beyond their standard limit of alcohol due to the weekend and the current Stanley Cup final. I make a break for it and don't look back.

I drift in and out of consciousness as I walk towards the city of Abbotsford. The country roads are long strips of flatlining fields. I start to craft ideas for a poem on my phone about Danielle amidst my active neurosis and melancholia. I'm about an hour into the walk when I get a ring on my phone. My oldest sister's partner, Jamie, who was also at my parent's party, heard about my whole situation and said he was coming to find me so I could safely get into town. He's right.

The chance of getting hit by a drunk driver on these unlit roads is relatively high. But I have already seen him drinking tonight. Was he one of them, too? I guess.

A few minutes pass, and I see his vehicle approaching from behind. I hop in and go over my situation with him.

Though my Sister, Tasha, and he are usually at each other's throats with heavy drama, deep down, I know he has good elements to his being. Jamie has survived being shot four or five times by Police, almost killing him. I know he's seen the worst of the worst and can relate to suffering through excess times of severe fucking lunacy.

I asked if we could hit the liquor store. He needed to restock, too. After replenishing our ammunition, he drops me off at the wooded area outside my friend's house. I'm still quite shell-shocked from my car accident a few hours ago, but I use the booze to guide me through the silhouettes of towering trees. Using the light of my phone, I embarrassingly stumbled upon the wrong house. I have been going to Chase's house for the last four years, but my state of mind is lost in the stars and lines me up in the backyard of his next-door neighbour. Ironically enough, Chase's

Mom is having a bonfire with the neighbours in their yard. She looks up at me, and I feel the surging waterfall of concern. It's clear she has observed the past maniacal bullshit I've found myself in, characterized by excessive partying and a lack of responsibility. She heard of my vehicular mess this afternoon and wondered why I never went to the hospital. I ignore it all, laughing it off. Chase finds me, holding a few beers in preparation, and we press on toward a night full of emptying the bottles in our mouths at a furious rate.

My earlier interrogation scene with death is almost entirely brushed off. No solvent exists capable of removing the neglect that has corroded my ego. The Final Sleep will linger a few feet away from here on out, watching me, waiting for a moment to strike from its unseen vessel every time I choose to dance with the bottle in hand.

Almost seven years later, I have learned nothing.

CHAPTER 4

Numb & Careless

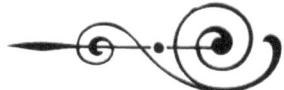

Early May 2018
Calgary, AB, Canada

I'm flooring it down 61st Ave in Calgary, Alberta, heading east in a pathetic attempt to believe I'll be making it to work today. I'm trying to correct the rearview mirror to meet my face. Am I at all presentable today? This always makes me laugh. I catch a glimpse of my eyes. They look like stamped, bloody dog shit. They look as if you froze the frames of the second a suicide jumper connected with the concrete after their brief contemplation on the way down to Earth. Even though they're naturally blue, they're crimson red and full of excremental mush.

I start to accelerate in fear. I take a swig of expensive Vodka. It looks like it was made in Sweden or someplace kissed by a Norwegian Iceberg. The tsunami of fragile butterfly wings ricocheting in my stomach, from the bottoms of my feet and up through my jittering hands. Orgasmic body tickles are blasted through the opening of a cannon with enough gunpowder to bury your average football stadium in a sea of explosive residue. The scent & taste of Vodka infiltrate every sense known to my spirit.

One hand on the wheel. One hand on the bottle. Always. 750ml of sky elixir filtrated through the purest of Angelic organs, processing its nectar into my bloodstream. A pair of Sugarskull cups clink & clang together on the passenger seat beside me. To my confusion, these gift items were included in the various bottles of alcohol purchased over the weekend. This is more evidence of what you acquire in a blackout state that seems to follow you for a little while.

White, speckled material is sprawled across my vehicle dashboard like dropping a bag of flour from the roof. I don't even do Cocaine. For a brief moment, I'm wondering if I finally gave in to other substances to keep me alive, but no. It's a heap load of Salt from the previous weekend of doing tequila shooters with a friend. Of course, a lot of drinking was done inside of a motor vehicle with zero care for any recourse. It could have been so much worse. For the most part, throughout the later courses of my career in Alcoholism, I carried a blanket of invisibility from local law enforcement while behind the wheel.

I had just moved to Alberta (from British Columbia) a few months back in an attempt to reformat my life. When I landed here, I dished out just $999 on a 1995 GMC Jimmy that had close to 400,000km on the Engine. The previous owner lied in the advertisement about the mileage, so I was able to knock him down a couple of bucks. The interior was like a miniature RV. There was enough room to pass out in the back (which one of my friends had done once as I drove around - him rolling around, entirely laid out, bouncing from side to side of the vehicle like the ball inside a Pinball machine). This whip was well insulated for the better parts of the slice & dice Winters that Alberta provides, but what did that matter if I was so juiced up all the time, ignoring temperatures, to begin with?

Back to reality.

Most of my thinking is entirely drawn & quartered due to the flood of vicious Death Metal blaring through the sound system my friend and I had drunkenly wired a month back. Butt connectors were exposed with a multitude of coloured spaghetti wires looking like it was all having sex with each other. It looked like a pair of five-year-olds were attempting first to discover the meaning of how electrical systems work. Once you reach a certain point of intoxication - that's exactly the age you devolve to. Men in their late 20's, mentally being transferred back to Pre-School. We speak the same. We act the same. We're just a little taller, heavier, and far more idiotic.

Realistically, I'll be arriving at work in five minutes, but I've already made up my mind down a different path. I cap off the Vodka and place it on the passenger seat while calling my boss. I've juggled a few ideas of bullshit in my mind to summon forth as a meaningful excuse for today's absence. He answers the phone.

"Hey, Jeff. I won't be able to make it in today," I say in my most awakened voice possible, "remember that toothache I had all week? Yeah. It's gotten worse, and I'm going to have it looked at

ASAP. Who knows. Maybe it could be an abscessed tooth, and things could get a lot worse from here."

"Oh shit, eh?" he laughs, "Fair enough! Go get that looked at, and we'll see you tomorrow."

I casually agree and hang up. I've verified with utmost precision that I will not be in tomorrow. Much like finding myself being lined up with five or six of my other comrades before a platoon of armed thugs, I've placed my back against the cold steel wall and faced the firing squad head-on. There's no turning back from this decision, and I'm well aware of the choice I've made. I pledge allegiance to the fine art of drunken lunacy. Where every decision that feels good at the time dawns a facade of a dopamine-coated blanket that reveals itself the following day as a hideous, demonic beast looking to rape you. From here on out - there is no threshold for destruction. No limit. I'll remain consumed in intoxication until I die.

Parking along the side of the road about a kilometre from my work, I call one of my best friends, Matthew, knowing he's already well on his way into the liquor.

"Hey buddy," I yell, in a trademark way as most of our conversations start, "what the fuck is going on over there?"

Matthew and I have been joined at the liver since 2012, when he began dating my older sister, Taylor. Throughout their relationship, it turned out that our friendship proved to be the valorous victor, rising tall to our true roots of mass partying, rowdy shit-disturbing lunacy, and letting the musical notes pour out of each slit in our skin from the unexpendable meteors of life's throes. After Taylor and Matt broke up in 2014, that allowed us to maximally further our antics without interference from anyone who wasn't a part of our delirious duo of destruction. A Brother for Life; metaphorically speaking, we cheers so hard that the glass bottles will forever shatter and lacerate our hands, with zero care of the blood spilled from roof to floor.

We chitchat for a few minutes, having *phone drinks* at 10 am and laughing about our typical subject matters of insanity. I ask where he's at and if he wants to get together to commit mass murder to our own lives. He tells me he's in town at another friend's house, just about to have a small house party this early in the morning. This is just how we roll. I stop and think for possibly five seconds about my choices. I throw the address onto my GPS. I pull a 180 on the road with G-Force weighing me down from the speed. I make my way over to this party house.

I sense it. I feel it. I do not want to bleed out and struggle through slaving to a 40/45 hour work week when all of this synergistic beauty between alcohol and the mind lays itself out to me in such bright colours. There is no turning back. There is a lack of responsibility. Such juvenile aggravation is brought on by the tendency to escape internal issues by tattooing them with a recipe for liver failure.

It takes me 30 minutes to arrive at this random residential neighbourhood. Along the way, I stopped at a gas station to grab some Sprite to mix into my Vodka. Why prolong the torture of the insanity when I can at least make it taste a little sweeter? For novelty, I arrive at the front door with the previously mentioned SugarSkull Cups in my truck and my hands full of Pop & Vodka. Let the fucking games begin.

There's nothing entirely new about this moment in time. The predictable banter of a group of alcoholics discussing what their lives used to be could have been and should have been. There are about seven or eight of us analyzing our musical choices, the bands we used to be in, and putting on random tunes that stretch across a multitude of genres. In usual fashion, I tend to be the one more associated with *extreme* music, but I'll be able to relate to pretty much anything, as I've listened to, studied and performed music for the last 14 years (at the time). Though he is nowhere near the brother level of Matthew and me, my other buddy, Tyler, puts on a hilariously offensive extreme metal band. No one else seems to enjoy it but him and I. I remind him that I made it on an album released in Mexico in tribute to these guys. This is more reason to celebrate our current senselessness. We all cheer to the loud ruckus, clang our glasses to the wave of flashbacks induced by tunes from younger years, and pick apart key elements of random band's choices on why they did this or why they did that. In many ways, these are some of the happiest moments of my life with the people I feel most comfortable around. Restricted from social chains due to the loosening inebriation, standing with those who suffer from the same character defects, and those educated enough about understanding how Music works - the prominent role it plays in commandeering our lives through the Forests of Folly. Even the arguments that break out from personal taste indifferences are in good spirits and usually coat the conversations with more razzle-dazzle. This is all, once again, brought upon by our nefarious nemesis - Booze. This continues until I hit the blackout switch in a random bedroom, still attached to this house.

Waking up from the soul-suppressing elements of the endless beers, vodka shots, and god knows what else, Matthew walks into the room with his phone. Like preschoolers, we spend another hour or so on the floor, losing our minds in hysterics from inside jokes, laughing at subjects that make no sense - the key to some of our humour that will live on until we pass. With a few brief pauses between laughter, we start to realize our arsenal of alcohol is running out. It's only 4 pm - usually when regular folk would consider going to the Liquor Store. I've been there once in the morning and feel zero shame returning. I would go a third or fourth time if needed. Matthew didn't take his vehicle here. We hop in my Jimmy and make a break for the LC. My logic at this moment is that one won't get caught as quickly for drinking and driving at these hours. No road checks or Police are looking for drunk drivers at 4 pm. What kind of sick person would be doing that, let alone be this intoxicated at this time of day (insert eye-rolling emoji)? After we arrive & exit from the store, the night turns into an overwhelming mist I'll be trapped in for weeks.

We spend the next seven or eight days at Matt's parent's apartment, drinking straight from the bottle like newborns would from their mother's breast. It's a two-bedroom duplex-style apartment that (thankfully) has two floors. His Parents understand our *conditions,* and we do our best to respect their privacy and keep our rambunctiousness out of the house, or at least kept to a quiet downstairs. There is food nearby, but consuming it is scarce. If there is any consumption of it, it's often the greasiest of hamburgers and the anti-health choices of sodium-overloaded noodle packages or pub food. Regardless, it usually all comes up regurgitated out of the mouth the next morning.

We are friends who share laughter, tears, struggles, and a bit of madness. Every morning that arrives feels like a sledgehammer striking my body. Two hardcore drinkers consume alcohol to dull the issues they've created, or when there are no significant problems, they muddle through confusing dilemmas and end up playing the blame game with someone else.

Throughout this bender, I found myself passed out in multiple areas around the apartment.

On the floor level, there is a fancy swimming pool that we dive into each night. This may have kept us feeling more rejuvenated and on our feet as the days passed.

It's hard to call a run to the liquor store a *run* when it's more like a *flail and fall*.

During one of these exhibitions, I keep bumping into the same cashier at the checkout. She's a cute, punky/gothic-looking girl who shyly gives me the flirty vibes every morning I pass through. I obtain an unbelievable amount of gall to think she's into me at all due to my apparent intoxication, lack of sleep, lack of hygiene, and lack of ordinary human functioning skills, but I press on. Leaving the store, Matt waits outside, sitting on a barricade in the parking lot. I tell him of this girl and hand him his bottle of booze. He mocks me in a way for not *manning up*, calling me a *pussy* for not trying to get her number. This pisses me off. In a rare action, due to my sober social anxiety and invisible drive, I march back into the store, booze still in hand, and ask for her number.

I'm immediately expecting failure & denial. With the amount of exhaustion and pain that's already circulating around my core - I don't care what the outcome is. Her eyes light up, and she writes her phone number on the back of a random receipt. I feel like I've just conquered the unconquerable. A gunless soldier rising from a wartorn beach towards victory. A real martyr for the suffering douchebag who commits to these kinds of acts every day of their lives. In an attempt to be humorous, I exit the store with both of my arms in the air, cheering loudly. I know she can still hear & see me. Matthew and I march onward to nowhere, clutching our liquor bottles like it's all we've got left.

We spent this day strolling the town drunk as all hell, making prank phone calls, stumbling around restaurants/bars and making it our mission to exist aimlessly without purpose. We sit on grassy hills around town, ranting and raving. Often, our conversations are on the brink of pure but fractured brutality. The kind of discussions that might get me locked up for years. This is the enjoyment of having a best friend; you don't need to feel filtered. These things need to be discussed, even with the contents of Alcohol playing its mischievous role in extracting the most vile of deprivation out of the soul. There's no time limit or set goals while in active alcoholism. Time is only a sightless currency when the store opens and when it's about to close. Maybe we get tired of daydreaming about being able to hook up with our waitress at the bar. Perhaps we're on suicidal autopilot mode. Regardless, we make it back to home base and retire to our regular spot by the swimming pool downstairs.

The night has fallen. Will I even lift my head to check if the Moon will provide some glow into this insanity? I find myself floating near the pool's deep end, looking into the empty workout room beside me. The Pool temperature is a tolerable warmth reflecting the spring weather outside, but a graven blanket of ice swings between my temples. Dim lights around the room's windows give the impression of a dreaded horror scene about to take place. In a haunting display, like bodies being granted access inside of a graveyard to be launched ten feet into the air suddenly, I witness a small child in the room beside me, tossing itself around in some epileptic fit.

"Jesus Christ," I blurt out, avoiding getting water in my mouth, "Do you see that, dude?! Why is there a little girl in there at this time?"

"No?" Matt questions, "The fuck are you talking about?"

It could have been how the lighting had balanced itself through the rods & cones in my eyes, but I started to witness a dark figurine of a child ravaging about in this visually apparent room. I get out of the water and stand against the pool wall, trying to conclude where I was.

I've read about Alcoholic Hallucinosis a few months ago in documented medical research. Maybe it's finally time this came to my mental doorstep. Moments like these are kept in an internal vault with such sentimental value that even the most horrific of images can obtain a glimmer of beauty. A few minutes go by, and the child disappears. She was just a wisp of miscalculated cerebral overload. Was she my *Pink Elephant* that other heavy drinkers have reported throughout history? I suddenly try to dawn a labcoat and analyze it with Matthew, but we're both too far gone to even care about the severity of this.

I will later study how this complication is often born from long-term, heavy alcohol abuse messing with the limbic system. This spawns a variety of auditory or visual hallucinations, creating havoc on the body's sensory systems and how it receives neural information. Never would I have heard of any of these warnings at a younger age before picking up such a destabilizing, murderous chemical. I wish I would have known.

This experience pushed me back against a barricade. I mention to Matthew that I'm freaked out and would like to head to bed. We dry off and exit the pool room. A couple of crooked steps take us to an elevator. The way back up to the apartment is void of noise. Even heavily sedated from these endless mud puddles of all that is alcohol, I'm still feeling anxious. Alcohol often removes all states of anxiousness, no matter what the outcome. Tonight is a bizarre fluctuation of unease. I feel like my life is deteriorating, and I'm simply just watching it unfold. It's a game of Russian roulette where the chamber is full. There is no chance of an empty cartridge. A 6/6 outcome of cranial fluid being sent the way of incendiary force. I used to have such a relentless fight for success. Where did it go? Was I possessed?

I make it to the downstairs floor of Matt's apartment. I shut the lights off, ensure some booze is left for me in the morning, and fade into the carpet.

Rise. Please keep anything from shining. Drink.

One of us, I can't remember who returns from the liquor store with a 40 of Vodka. We're both running out of money, but neither of us is willing to admit to any faults or wrongdoings. We're getting a little restless with each other after spending over a week partaking in voluntary suicide. Who wouldn't? Boundaries are essential for all social plants to evolve appropriately. Our friendship was becoming drained of all nutritional value. Nothing worthwhile is harvested from investing time together, puppeteered by the holy decimator that is Alcohol.

One of us suggests we bring a girl or two over. I've been texting the one who worked at the Liquor store back and forth. She was eager to come over and have a few casual drinks. She had absolutely no clue what would have been in store for her liver (and mind). I'm thrilled she never ended up coming over. Eventually, one of my other friends, Meg, responded to a juvenile mass text message I sent out, bleeding for attention. She lives roughly 25 minutes away on the east side of town. We make plans to hit the pool downstairs and bring on a third member to our adventure to the bottom of this abysmal existence.

Matt and I are standing on the balcony of this 8th-floor apartment building, looking out towards the west section of Calgary, Dalhousie. I get a text from Meg that she is downstairs with no money after she has taken a taxi here. Matt heads down to the bottom floor to pay for it. Still standing on the balcony, I notice the two on the ground floor. I'm taking in how high this building is. I never adopted a fear of heights, but rather, my mind took on the intrusive thoughts of how much of a significant disadvantage I would be if I fell off this deck.

A few minutes pass, and the two return to the room. Matthew's attitude has gone from a person I've known for years to an incredibly cocky and arrogant *bro* character. Regardless of the booze playing Minesweeper in my head, it's pretty clear to me he's trying to act tough in front of Meg in a weird state of intimidation and arrogance. After spending too many nights in this apartment, it's starting to bother me. Both of us being inebriated to the high heavens does not help any of this. Stack on sleep deprivation and a thirst for death - we begin to clash like a shitty romantic B movie over a girl we don't know much about. I've known Meg for six weeks. He's known her for maybe three. There's a barrage of screaming and yelling. I make murderous eye contact with Matthew. I don't know who he is. He's thinking the same about me. This is one of my Brothers in Arms, who I've barrelled down the destructive corridors of life with. Now, he's become the opposite. He throws a punch. I'm rocked with a pretty stiff right hand that almost puts me out. A handful of seconds go by, and I'm on top of him, raining down hammer fists into his skull. We grapple and are launched around the house. After a bonding week between the two of us, these sorts of dilemmas seemed impractical, but not when Alcohol is the culprit and cattle prod behind the madness. Meg is screaming for her life in confusion and fear. I'm juiced up with adrenaline, as is Matthew. It doesn't last too long, but enough to invoke damage on both of our faces. Both of us are like delirious lions rolling on a Safari with poachers tasing our bodies.

Someone, either from the next room or god knows where calls the Police. A handful of minutes pass, and an entire Cop Squad is present in the apartment. I'm thinking I'm going to spend the night in jail, but things pan out a different way. I've physically lost sight of where Matthew went. He had made it to the lobby downstairs when we separated from each other. These last few minutes are filled with blurred yells. I notice the Police with their hands on their weapons, ready to just pepper me. I sort of come back to reality and begin talking to one of the officers. What upsets me the most is seeing a Vase smashed against the wall. The vase belonged to Matthew's parents. After the hospitality they showed me and the delightful presence they've always been around me, I honour them by bringing violence into their household. The violence could have been much worse, but that is not the point. I left my statement. I'm disgusted with myself. One of the officers leads me out of the apartment and chats with me in the elevator.

"Your other friend is downstairs. Please do not speak or make any motions towards him. We will take action if you do."

The elevator doors slide open, revealing Matthew sitting upright on a couch in the lobby, surrounded by other officers. He seems relatively more collected than I am, myself still overflowing with untamed primal rage.

"FUCK YOU, ASSHOLE!" I scream with both of my middle fingers in the air towards him. The cops do nothing. It crossed my mind that that little gesture could have gotten me charged, but even with the warning... I didn't care. It only amplified how distraught I was—lack of coherence. Meg followed me on the way down. We're now standing outside with three or four police cruisers surrounding the front of the building. Most of these Officers were probably hoping the noises Matt and I made were part of an actual murder scene. We could have given them some flesh tossed around in colourful fashion like a Southern Texas chainsaw-wielding hillbilly was drinking with us. A pinata full of plasma. Something to bring back to the office and rave about with other staff. All they got were two shirtless maniacs reeking of dysfunction and strong Vodka.

Meg and I trudge onward, away from the Police. We walk a few blocks down towards the city. My face feels like I kneeled before a professional baseball player and asked him to swing at the front of my head as if his career depended on it. I look up and see the illuminated restaurant lights of Boston Pizza. It's around 7 pm, and I'm thirstier than ever before. It's open. They serve Alcohol. That's all I care about. I've stayed coherent for this entire day, nestled in the fluid that keeps me so lively, so what's a little more going to do? After this whole fist-fighting fiasco, the adrenaline propels me to pound back the sauce with death-like intensity. The two of us walk into the restaurant and sit at the bar. I realize I have a few hundred dollars left on my Visa that I thought I had maxed out. I order shots. We slam them. I guzzle them back like an empty fuel pump, craving waves of Octane.

CHAPTER 5

Angel Rust

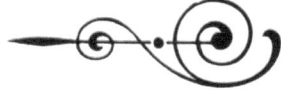

One of my Best Friends and I have just beaten the shit out of each other on the balcony of his Parent's 8th-floor apartment. The view from this perch indicated any fall would staple our Death Certificates to the wall of the closest Morgue to our drop point. Is this where we believe in Miracles? Was it a Miracle that neither of us fell off to our fateful end? In some instances, you can believe in this phenomena and how they happen and guide us away from torment & ill-will, but in all honesty - it's just the unpredictable nature of how Alcohol weaves its thorn-based web. Maybe it would have been a lot nicer if both of us fell together, and for the brief period of descending to the parkade below, I could have given him one last hug and said,

"Thank you for being there for me." It is a sort of honourable way for two rambunctious lunatics to put an end to dragging everyone down with them. The only thing dragging with us was the mere physics of gravity. We would no longer be lost; a newly discovered permanent resting place would have been found.

My phone is more dead than my apparent life's source. Typically, a phone depleted of its power causes an unmeasurable amount of dread & panic, but my current state deferred all of that. I use what's left on my Visa to buy the landslide of shots at the tabletop Bar. Both of us are still stuck here at Boston Pizza. I don't know if Meg has a proper house to return to. I could haul it back to my place, but it's twice the distance across town. Plus, I don't feel like spending this night alone. When I'm drunk, my Oxytocin levels tend to stir (almost crazily) on the higher side. When I'm sober, I struggle to feel much of a physical connection with others. Tonight, I focus on rekindling with my teddy bear side.

I ask one of the bartenders to call a cab for us. Thirty minutes pass, and no taxi has arrived.

"Did you even call us a cab, buddy?" I drunkenly spit at the Bartender.

"Yes," he politely responds, "it's probably just a busy night. Chill out."

For no reason at all, I've negatively targeted this man for courteously helping me out here. Another 25 minutes went by, and our delivery vehicle finally arrived. I throw another rude remark over to the bartender; he tosses one back. Maybe he wasn't quite feeling my vibe as I initially walked into the bar looking the way I did. Bruised face. Ripped flannel jacket. Dress shoes. It seems like I was rejected from the Circus. I briefly remember trying to walk in with no shirt on, too. That doesn't often work in a public setting. Things start to make sense as I walk out, flipping him the bird. Meg follows me, and we collapse into the cab. We head back to her house half an hour across town.

The week that follows is condensed into a grimy den of compost and wreckage. I think I've showered once in the last 14 days. Meg has now replaced Matthew for taking turns annihilating the bottle in a gruesome fashion. She is just as dedicated to self-destruction as I am. Being a cute & petite girl of her size, I have no clue how she can keep up with me. I'd say she's 5'2 and weighs 100 pounds. I'm nearly 6'4 and at 215lbs. Somehow, Meg makes it to work for a few days, even though we've been on this degrading mission to partake in the games of debauchery. Each morning's shaking sessions are getting worse & worse. I'm slit open from the front of my stomach up to my face via tremors and unexplainable body twitching that only goes away by keeping more alcohol down. Meg is not on my addiction level (yet). She's five years younger than me, giving her nervous system a much healthier outlook than mine. It's not so torn in two. Mine is consistently tied with razorwire, being toyed around in salt water above a school of Tiger Sharks. The few days Meg is off to her job, I'm left to combat my demise around her two-story townhouse. While my situation is god-awful - I feel terrible for her. Imagining her working with a crippling hangover floods me with anxiety. I used to voluntarily suffer through that for years.

The nearby liquor store doesn't open until 10 am—one of the most baffling & chaotic creations known to man. No

Alcoholic should have to wither around with his intestines exposed, watching the clock ticking slowly. We should be able to get our supply at any moment's notice. This feeling is pulverizing. Each second comes at me, brandishing various weapons. It feels like brushing my teeth with a switchblade. My ignorance lights the wick of my life, and it's curling around to a barrel of TNT. I wish I were back in British Columbia for the sole reason of stores opening an hour earlier. This thought puts me in a mental chokehold. The panic rises. Will I survive the countdown, or will Meg return home to find me in a few hours, already dead on her floor?

Like after a rainstorm of mediocre proportions, there are tiny bits of alcohol left in some of the bottles around Meg's house. I collect them like a desperate fool, pouring half vodka into half whisky and small amounts of coolers back into the vodka. I pay little attention to detail and try not to investigate the contents too profoundly. It has booze in it - that's all that matters. I drink it, sometimes plugging my nose so I don't spew my stomach bile around the room like a water balloon that's too full of fluid. All of this feels like forcing a kiss onto somebody you've stopped loving. Endless shame. All of this guilt, but those few shots of straggler booze resurrect me from my flirtatious swindling with Death. I'm starting to mentally blend back into coherence, but not physically. My body feels as if I tried carving out my organs with a Swiss Army Knife (specifically with that tiny corkscrew) to sell on the black market. The dull but searing pain of these last few weeks is appearing to take its toll. At this point and where my financial status was heading/bleeding, perhaps selling my organs was in my best interest; I don't believe my Liver would be highly sought after, though.

I flop down the stairs to the first floor of Meg's house and notice a whole fleet of House Cats. Felines of different shapes and sizes. An average Orange cat (usually the most arrogant of these hellions), a monstrous Norwegian Forest Cat that looks like he dabbled in the Mane Coon gene pool, and another cat of the latter family who's relatively more minor than the previous big-haired thug. The kitchen is relatively clean. Meg evidently has a roommate who's in the house, as the agenda of the last few nights between the two of us has been everything but sanitary. Maybe these Cats do all the maid services around the house? All of this seems trivial. I need to stock up on booze.

I type in *liquor store* on the Maps App on my Phone. The GPS lights up, and it shows only 500M from here. I was on edge, thinking I'd have to summon the strength to walk 5km. God, this is perfection. My mood flips to another channel. I'm licking my lips with excitement for another bottle.

My phone was plugged in all night (probably from Meg), as when I'm internally this wrecked, I often forget to charge it, usually breaking the charging cable in the process.

All I've got for clothing is my work pants, which I left the house with two weeks ago, and my steel-toed work shoes. If I tried to wear one of Meg's shirts - I'd rip it in the process as we share an almost foot-and-a-half difference in height. The *No shirt, no shoes, no service* policy starts to scare the shit out of me. I need this goddamn bottle. Therefore, I need a shirt. I'm beginning to think I could just wrap a towel around my body and walk in like this.

Maybe a blanket? A full garbage bag? If I'm buying alcohol this early in the morning, does it even matter what anyone would think of me, regardless? Holy fuck - I'm going to look ridiculous. I limp back up to Meg's room and search her closet for an oversized shirt. I find a long-sleeved band shirt, possibly from another guy she was seeing, and throw it on. Taking a few seconds to catch my breath, I'm out the door, with one last look behind me, making sure the cats don't follow.

Exiting the house, I lose my WiFi connection and realized Siri lied to me.

As I follow the path toward where my treasure awaits, there is a massive, fortified, seven-foot-high fence surrounding the vicinity of this complex. I have no time to try and bullshit with my phone to stare at a map and figure out how to get out of this substantial fort-like residence. I make a quick decision to stand on a nearby boulder, grab the tops of the fence and do a frontflip over while letting out a banshee-style yell. I'm not a tiny, condensed person. My limbs are long and swing freely. This must have looked hilarious to the passerby. I crash down on the opposite side of the fence onto straight concrete. I just about ruptured my spleen. Maybe it did happen. The pain multiples as I try to stand, but the thought of acquiring more alcohol prods me with a quick painkiller. The Liquor store was just on the other side of the fence, so I'd already made it to my destination. This is all too dangerously close in proximity to be living beside. Lock, stock and packing the pistol with an endless supply of ammunition to bring down all the luxuries of life, I enter the store and am granted one more day of inebriated freedom.

To what extent of weight can the Human mind repel before snapping like the crispiest of twigs found on a frigid January morning? I push the boundaries of that question and find myself stretching it out for a total onslaught of two to three weeks at a time. Each bender becomes more costly on all fronts (mentally, financially, and physically). Still, right now, I'm on about day thirteen and finding a strange internal obelisk trying to guide me toward a better understanding. This routine of sacrificing jobs and dragging my name through the bubbling tar of oil puddles in Hell has made me entirely fed up and obliterated by my dismal menu of an endless alcoholic waterfall.

The last few days are an opening of the liquor taps only to black out a few hours afterwards—morning, day, night. Meg and I drink with all the time allowed to us and repeat day after day, night after night. No new news is rolling in on the vessel of my life other than that it will come to a grotesque halt in a body bag if I don't do something hastily about it. After another monumental peak withdrawal blitz of anxiety, panic, and derealization - I use the morning Alcohol consumption to bring me back to feeling like I'm nestled beside a small bonfire of warmth. The option of Rehab enters an area of my brain that hasn't been active in years. The area that lights up where responsibility was once flourishing.

It's mid-morning, nearing the end of the week. Meg has left for work. I'm gone to painstakingly roll around in her bed, feeling the illness return in its vicious wake. Half a 2'6 (750ml) of Vodka is on the ground. It's like an internal fire alarm has detected a wave of soul-swallowing heat and requires hard alcohol to douse the flames. After a few minutes of shooting back vodka & maintaining no projection of my stomach lining making its way through my teeth onto the floor, I'm able to hold my phone correctly as the shakes subside. During this moment of stabilization, I talk to Matthew on the phone again. We make amends and come to terms with how fucking stupid we act when we drink (as we apologize, we continue to drink). I come to my senses and wipe the chalkboard clean of nonsensical, drunken equations. It's time to check myself into Rehab immediately.

I search for *Alcohol Rehabilitation nearby* in Google and am blown in half with results that could roll on for years. The amount of clinics in North America is more than staggering. These are foundations with deep-rooted fundamentals at the core of business. Patients are clients. The addiction is their valued fodder. Desperate souls on the brink of suicide or deterioration of the working heart muscle are their trees to the lumber yard. I have enough money to fly anywhere in the world to undergo at least a month of treatment. My pair of dice landed on a small facility on Vancouver Island in the city of Nanaimo (which is relatively closer to my current position compared to Texas, Quebec, Hawaii, or Florida). I dial a number presented to me on screen and chat with one of the facilitators. The person over the phone seems willing to help, but I might have to wait two to three weeks to get in.

I arrogantly decline the waiting process and force my hand into the conversation. I tell them I have tens of thousands of dollars and want to curb this addiction as soon as I can. Their tone changes. They become more compassionate and understanding. Typical. The evergreen glisten of the Dollar Bill is essentially a magic wand for all bogus charitable transactions. One of their intake buildings is here in Calgary, and I agreed to meet them tomorrow for a documented session. I have no clue how I'll be able to get there, but I'll deal with that once the time shows itself. This leaves me with another 24 hours to reign supreme in the world of alcoholic chaos.

I make a Facebook post to the world, to my family and friends, that I'm off to repair the links that once held my life intact before Alcoholism so destructively raped them. In my Facebook post, I record a 30-second video. I look horrendous. Pale, tired, out of shape, and sporting a lovely black eye from the fight with Matt a week ago. I'm almost spitting rocks from how gravelly my voice sounds. I finish the remainder of the Vodka left in the house. I head outside toward the liquor store, trying to drink the light out of the sky with an imaginary straw to allow my body to remember what it feels like to have any sliver of brightness on the inside.

The following day churns its horridly disfigured face as I scrape my hair from the toilet bowl. Looking like spilled radioactive material from a nuclear powerplant, my stomach bile is glowing amongst the sides of the porcelain. Emerald lime. Citrine gut-rot. Speckled opal with enough potently rancid reek to form blisters on the insides of your nose. My hand is so far down my throat, getting rid of yesterday, trying to pull some kind of relief back into my life.

Today is the day to carve a new exit away from all of this.

I collect myself from the ground and fall back into bed where Meg is lying. We cuddle for a bit. She tells me how proud she is that I'm taking these steps. She's given me a place to stay for over a week, but I know that being here is allowing me to sign out of my physical body far too early. This has to end, or all of this is over.

I allow myself only to consume a smaller portion of Vodka before I venture off to undergo my intake session for rehab. This will be a crucial mistake, and I will heavily pay the price for it.

I catch a taxi to Downtown Calgary and locate the facility where an intake worker is waiting to assess the amount of damage I've done to myself. From that point on, I don't remember much except expressing my frustration with my ongoing struggle with alcoholism and hoping that the place he works for can help me get back on my feet.

He takes a moment to observe my appearance and the fatigue etched on my face. Concern fills his eyes as he asks, "How are you going to manage the journey from Calgary to Nanaimo in this state?" (roughly 1,100km apart with an ocean in between).

"I will sort out a fucking plan," I assure him, "even if it means I have to fly there tonight."

Gripped by this full wash of a manic tidal wave, I sign some papers, shake the guy's hands, and head toward the Calgary airport.

Before people head to rehab, they often bring a few bags of belongings and personal items to help them exist in their newly acquired setting. They are usually ushered in by family or work. Most importantly, they are often appropriately detoxed off of whatever they're struggling with. Not me. I have nothing, nobody, and I still have what's killing me in my bloodstream—an immediate three strikes. I am a lacerated solitary wolf wandering through the northern wilderness, skin exposed to the acidic winds.

I show up at the airport looking as awful as I have ever looked in my life: hair all over the place, bruised face, steel-toed work shoes, ripped dress pants, and a flannel jacket. A destroyed wardrobe of a drifting clown. Some might even laugh at this, but I'm in no comedic mood. I've only had a small amount of liquor this morning and can feel myself already spinning wildly out of control. I went from consuming litres of hard alcohol for weeks to a minimal amount this morning. Though this is not essentially *cold turkey*, reducing alcohol consumption even by a small amount, after prolonged periods of excess, is enough to send someone's body into life-altering states of withdrawal. As I approach the lineup to purchase airplane tickets, I'm just about rocked out of my fucking shoes with a sharp jolt inside my shoulders. I feel my body stiffen as I try to grab onto the railings that lead me to the ticket booth. Everything around me is doused with a blurring blanket. I quietly gasp for air and stumble backwards towards a bench that's against the wall. My heart is fluttering so fast that it feels like nothing is inside of my ribcage. The people around me are transforming into radiating blobs of energy. I have no clue but to phone 911. The dissociation has me feeling like I'll be having a stroke in less than 5 seconds. Thankfully, the ambulance is quick on the draw. On cue, a rush of men come to my side and check my pulse; it's well over 200 bpm, sputtering randomly offbeat like a jazz musician about to overdose on crack. A different paramedic checks my blood pressure; it's over 220/130. I'm utterly paralyzed with fear, believing I could die at any moment. Due to all of these high readings, they put me on a stretcher and get me to the hospital at lightning speed.

On the drive over, though I hear and feel death scraping its nails on the chalkboard, I'm able to give them my story, how I'm trying to quit drinking after undergoing a brutal few weeks of debauchery. I'm still coherent, but I feel I could pass out any second. Some of the symptoms are spiking at painful rates. Through all of this, I'm still committed to going to rehab. I reminded the nurses & staff that I have to get to Vancouver Island by tomorrow morning.

A few hours pass, and I'm discharged. They were able to calm my body down from the withdrawal by administering Lorazepam. This curbs most of the symptoms in under 30 minutes. Lorazepam (otherwise known as Ativan) is a part of the Benzodiazepine class of drugs that produces a mirroring calming effect on the brain in relation to Alcohol. It is the paramount and sought-after first line of defence (or attack) against Alcohol Withdrawal. When titrated and given correctly, it is often a quick cure against moderate symptoms. Although the experience was downright excruciating and left me reeling (and it will progress to become worse eventually), all has passed. As I'm released, a Doctor supplies me with a care package: six more Lorazepam for my journey. "Listen," he says firmly, his gaze piercing, "only take these if you notice any of the symptoms coming back." Those words go through one ear and out the other.

Again, I find myself hailing a taxi to the airport in record time. As I approach the booth to purchase tickets, one of the attendants recognizes me from the incident a few hours ago. A bit of commotion is stirred as they are hesitant to let me board a plane after undergoing what I just went through. I assure them that I will not be an issue, even producing a slip from the hospital showing I've been discharged and am well enough to fly. It takes a few minutes, but they eventually allow me through.

I'm waiting past the security point for my airplane to board, luggage-less and propped up on a seat in the ill-fitted terminal waiting area. Hundreds of people stroll by, yet I still feel marooned, mentally succumbing to vicious misanthropy. I still have an hour or so to kill. Choosing to add relief to these escapades, I take two of the Ativan prescribed to me. I did this exact thing in New York just five months prior and was able to keep myself together to board the plane, free of anxieties. Only this time, I'll be consuming far too much alcohol.

I look up and am lulled by the sights & sounds of a small airport bar in the distance. The allure of the drinks being poured is drawing me closer and closer. If going into a stupor that eventually leads to your death is on your bucket list, mixing Benzodiazepines with heavy alcohol use will cross that off the chart in no time. Pulled uncontrollably toward the vicissitude, I find myself attached to a barstool. I lose count of how many jagerbombs and beers I'm able to drink in under an hour. The way the bartender allows me to keep drinking despite my dishevelled appearance is truly astonishing. Maybe it's the caffeine from the Redbull that keeps my body awake to enable it to float like a ripped map on a lake littered with chaotic waves. My last clear memory is of an announcer's voice echoing through the terminal, calling for my flight's boarding. After that, it all becomes a blur—where hazy moments merge with the effects of countless drinks I've indulged in. I pop the rest of the remaining Ativan into my mouth, which equates to four final tablets. All I recall is the dim corridor leading to the airplane entrance. A blackout sweeps over my consciousness. My body and mind sink deeper into a haze, edging me closer to a state of near-death—an abyss of nothingness engulfed in a pitch-dark freefall.

CHAPTER 6

We're on the Wrong Island

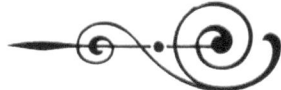

<u>**Mid-May 2018**</u>
<u>**Vancouver Island, Nanaimo, B.C., Canada**</u>

B leeding light returns. Rows of mirror-like glass architecture flow across the roof ceiling. I blink at a steady pace to assure myself that this is reality. Scarce were the visions or dreams collected in the last 12 hours. I quickly notice I'm on a hospital gurney with a few IV needles in my arm. My previous collection of memories was of walking down an entrance hallway to board a plane from Calgary to Nanaimo. Thinking this might be the rehab center I tried getting to, I take a glimpse around the room. Nothing indicates I safely made it to my destination. Did I even get on the Airplane? Did they deny me, and somehow, I woke up back in Alberta? Did I board the wrong flight and am now somewhere else in the World?

A Nurse appears through the curtains in front of me.

"Good morning, Jordan," she calmly greets me, "You're lucky to still be here with us."

"What the hell happened? Am I in Alberta still?" I confusingly ask her.

"No," she assures me, "You're on Vancouver Island. You were found unconscious on the floor of the airport here."

The combination of a weight-filled consumption of Alcohol on top of the Ativan I had taken almost ceased the operation of my brain to remind my lungs to keep breathing.

A micro-sliver of imagery tries to pour all over me. The airport carpet returns to mind, but I don't know if I'm just imagining things. Nothing makes sense.

I'm left flabbergasted that I was able to board the flight, let alone leave it after the in-flight experience. The fact of cheating death once more barely stays with me before it burrows through my bones and hides dormant in the farthest reaches of my cells to come and say *"hi"* later on in life.

"We've kept in contact with one of the facilitators at the rehab facility you were trying to get to," the nurse debriefs me, "they will be here to pick you up in a few hours."

Not knowing whether I'm in the city of Nanaimo or one of the smaller surrounding cities, I prepare myself for a bumpy ride toward sobriety. All I'm aware of is trying to get to the Rehab Centre.

An hour passes, and I'm somehow barely able to stand tall from the previous night's slugfest. I wander outside. The oceanic

Vancouver Island air bubbles with a salty residue for all to behold. An SUV approaches and parks in front of me.

"You're alive!" jokes the driver of the vehicle, exiting his car and walking towards me.

"Apparently so," I retaliate, "I have no fucking clue where we're at right now, but I have a feeling you do."

This guy seems to possess an excess amount of energy that I'm not really in the mood for, but he's my chauffeur to safety, so I tolerate it for the time being.

Hopping in the passenger seat makes me feel as if I'm going to pass out. My body, mind and soul are in no shape to be enclosed in a vehicle and forced to undergo a windy adventure.

The entire ride towards Rehab, my head is against the window glass, trying to channel all ounces of calm left in my puzzle piece of a life that's been flipped violently, tossing thousands of its pieces across an uneven floor.

We arrive.

A middle-of-May rainstorm batters my face the second I step out of the car. My feet hit the ground; I immediately just want to lie down in the parking lot, calling one of the rain puddles my pillow for the night. The front entrance is littered with savoury flowers and attractive plants that have been prepared by a Gardener who appears to have the best form of OCD to date; it looks absolutely flawless. Never judging the book by its cover, I ignore the serene facade and enter through the front door.

I feel like I've just entered through a sightless forcefield full of swamps of fictitious compassion, semi-synthetic egos and a group of soul-draining white collars looking at addicts as a source of income and profit. I hold this belief with me for the entire time. I'm taken to the main lobby, where a wide variety of eyes I've never seen before gaze upon me.

Ranging from male to female, either 19 to 65, are the people I'll be seeing throughout my stay here. There are a few cute girls, your average Joe's, your typical jock-looking douchebags, some nerds, some hippies, and what is a Rehab center without your super sketchy-looking characters who, no matter how many days of sobriety they have under their belts, will always look like they just woke up in the middle of the street. Something about this reminds me of being in high school.

While being taken to the intake area, I vomit into a garbage can quickly given to me by some random female I'll never see again.

In the closed-off Intake room, I'm asked to strip down completely naked, tuck my scrotum upwards, and bend over, spreading my asscheeks while coughing, to show that I haven't brought any contraband in here with me. As I do this, I say to the guy that I don't have any problems with Drugs, just Alcohol. He laughs. This is the first time in my life that I've ever had to be completely naked in front of another grown man. The level of uncomfortable feelings is unchartable. I quickly put on my clothes and organized my banking information for the financial team for the initial days of my stay to avoid being kicked out immediately.

Things start out pretty god damn rough with most of my cylinders misfiring in improper combustion order. I stay in bed for two full days. Doing the bare essentials of math this month, my self-made chaos has had me partying for about 14 days in a row. My body was reminded that adequate sleep is still required to continue to exist. I briefly remember a nurse coming into my room a few times and giving me some medications to keep any severe withdrawal symptoms from connivingly appearing out of nowhere. By the third morning, I'm able to join the rest of the battered souls in the dining room for Breakfast. Those who have been here longer have a relatively brighter aura about themselves. I can immediately figure out who's a veteran and who's just beginning. Consider it a spruced-up and less dangerous version of Prison (not that I would know what that's like .. yet).

Noticeable are the irritating *bros* who feel like they have ownership of the entire place and that this is their "territory" to play. The tough guy bullshit doesn't vibe well with me, and with my first few minutes around specific characters, I'm already feeling homicidal.

For breakfast, we advance in a single file with our trays stretched outwards for chefs to place food onto. The food is A+, and I feel my appetite return like pleading with a sheet of clouds for heat, and the sun finally breaks through. Each table is separated into cliques and clowns. I hadn't taken the time to socialize with anybody, so I slumped over to a table by one of the girls, Gwen, who had tried talking to me when I first arrived. Her first words as she eyed me up and down were, "You're a hot fucking mess." This woman is the definition of badass, littered with random tattoos, ex-military, dropping F-bombs every second word but still emitting some type of charming complexion. I feel comfortable around her, so I slightly relax. While I mentioned the food was superb, I mismanaged my fragile digestive system. As I tried consuming breakfast, it came right back up out of my esophagus. I dart towards the side of the room, making it, running over to the garbage can, but not without smearing some of my dignity onto the floor. I hear a group of guys huddled at one table, laughing at my misfortunes. I want to turn around and kick one of them so hard in the head that I could play soccer with his brains for the next few days. I can't eat or partake in participating with humans. I'm brought back to my room, where I sleep another day. I can't tell if it's the medication they're giving me, but I'm piledriven with lethargy.

Day four brings an annoyingly familiar and optimistic facilitator to my door the next morning: it's the guy I had to strip down in front of.

"Hey Jordan," he says, smiling brightly, "are ya' feeling better? I'm here to collect some more money!"

I want to clothesline this guy into fucking oblivion or grab him by his goofy golf shirt and send him through the closest glass window. He's one of the leading managers here, so I comply and follow him back to his office. Earlier, while I was trying to put together my payments for a month's stay here, the effects of withdrawing and loss of sleep had me messing up all ounces of correct paperwork; they permitted me to pay for the first week in advance to begin detoxing correctly. Now that I'm relatively grounded, I fork over nearly $20,000 for my first month's stay. I've managed to hold onto half of what I made on my apartment sale in 2017, but after this transaction, there are only a few thousand dollars left in my savings. As the facilitator talks to me, I lose focus. I no longer walk with skin that will translate the workings of empathy back into reality. There's an unignorable disconnect. Understanding that I've pretty much sold my Apartment to spend on Rehab (that doesn't feel like it will work) places me outside the room of reality into the barren lands of psychopathy. Maim. Unhinge. Deface. Uncreate. Remove. So this is what it feels like to be on the edges of fateful wrath?

I walk out of the room and back to the lounging hall to try and distract myself from the financial loss I've endured. I should be looking at this as a positive gain toward sobriety, but my attitude is too fresh away from the bottle, lacking any common grounds with apparent cognitive functioning. I imagine all of the better times I could have had with that money. My plans on staying here long aren't in the picture, so I'm left with a stranded and helpless state of affairs.

Though it's in none of my genuine interest, I am able to bond with most of the people stuck here with me, the only real friends being Gwen and another artistic, creative soul named Sam. Sam, being from Vancouver, talks like there are a million visually artistic ideas encircling him all at once. I often feel this way musically so there's a bit of a bond being formed.

On my fifth day here, I politely ask to leave and am denied. I've straight up been told that I'm not thinking correctly and to go to one of my meetings for reassurance. Though I follow their orders, I immediately feel trapped and cornered by bureaucratic douchery. Am I doing the right thing by wanting to leave? Are they the conveyors of truth? These absolute strangers who just want to suck me dry of the money I've earned over the years. How many other people are they doing this to?

Once you sign up for Rehab, remember that your bank account is what keeps the place afloat. They will do all in their power to have access to it from here on out. For no apparent reason, due to poorly managed facilitating, I'm placed into a group of people who have come clean with their sexual addictions. As someone who just struggles with Alcoholism, I'm left to sit in a circle of six other Men who hash out their problems with Sex and its possessive nature. Addiction is addiction, but the desire for the bottle and the impulsivity towards uncontrollable sexual urges feel distant from one another (at least to me). One of the older gentlemen is speaking, sobbing like a child pulled out of Toys'R'Us too early by the hand of his Mother. He tells us all how he brought gonorrhea back to his Wife after sleeping with an endless amount of street-walking prostitutes. I close my eyes as he is speaking and imagine diving through the glass that leads to the surrounding Ocean outside. It's my turn to talk. I go off on a bit of a rampage, struggling to maintain words that don't resemble profane axe blows. The facilitator reminds me to restrict myself from said obscenities, but I continue my use of swearing, slightly with less emphasis on the initial sounds of cacophony. I try my best to keep my tongue in its jail cell for my own safety around these other Men. Being placed in this group besieges me with such an insecure boiling point of frustrating mental explosions. I should have packed my bags and begun the (long) walk to the airport right then and there.

The dull days and motorless nights slowly pass. For my sleeping situation, I'm paired in a room with a 60-year-old overweight guy from the East Coast who snores like a mystical sea creature flexing its vocal cords for other aquatic life to fear his wrath. Why they would put someone detoxing off of Alcohol into an absurdly loud room joined up with an elephant beats me. It goes on for far too many nights, rendering me to walk to the main office to ask for a different room. They put me in the chapel room, separated from the living quarters, which consists of a pull-out couch and an altar for prayer. The lustre of the Cathedral glass holds its glow, even in the night. It provides the soundless landscape required to nod off.

They don't allow me to sleep here for the next night, giving me earplugs and pretty much telling me to deal with it. Due to this, I sneak down the hallway into an empty room, awaiting the next incoming patient, and peacefully enter a slumber due to the peace of no other beings around me. The next morning, to avoid detection, I'm able to wake myself up half an hour before the rising bell of Dawn, making the bed that I'm leaving to sneak back into my assigned room. I don't take it seriously, but I've begun to undergo a series of troubling battles with sleep paralysis.. or is this the introduction to hallucinations caused by suppressed withdrawal? That morning, as my eyes opened to the morning light, I could see a group of Cats running to and fro around the room, with my blanket slightly levitating a foot above my body. Rubbing my eyes, they all disappeared, and my blanket returned to adhering to the laws of gravity. I brought this up to one of the nurses the next time we spoke. They can add it to my ever-growing folder of instability for the governmental overlords to use against me one day.

The end goal here in Rehab is to become reformed into the bedrock of society. Some individuals have had their children torn from their arms, some dealing with court cases that may land them in prison if they don't complete a full round of months-long therapy, and then there's me, a hardcore alcoholic who's just hellbent on maintaining his unorthodox lifestyle without political and hierarchal interference.

Most of our days are conducted by a pinheaded therapist, hosting four meetings of group therapy a day, waiting for someone to be done talking around the room so he/she can ask, *"How does that make you feel?"* at the end of every session. Come closer and ask that question so I can uppercut you through the roof tiles and towards Pluto. I cannot believe I'm paying close to $1,000 a day for this nonsensical bullshit. The more I listen to these preachers in disguise rehash their social rhetoric from wall to wall, the more I'm pushed backwards toward the exit sign.

During one of our full group meetings after lunch, Sam and I compare the tattoos we have, weaving quick stories behind them. One of our loudmouthed patrons reminds us that there is to be no cross-talk during these meetings. For a split second, I felt like hurling my sitting chair into the front of his skull, hoping a fiendish entity would have provided me pinpoint precision, breaking the front of his face into fragments. With each progressing day, my attitude becomes wartorn with escapism. I plan to make an exit soon.

We're allowed to go on supervised walks around the property every other day. I feel like there's a rifleman up in the watchtower watching all of us caged animals run about while he contemplates blindly shooting at us if we dare to venture offbounds. Myself and a group of other guys skip rocks across a dormant pond compiled at the end of the yard. I follow Gwen around and have now marked her as one of the only people I can trust within our zone of influence.

The Ocean is less than a Kilometre or so away. Micro-magnets in my skin are pulling themselves in the direction of each molecule of salt water in its vast, deep blue. It takes all of my strength not to run toward the smell of the water and want to plunge into it for eternity.

After I'm done with the pointless excursion of being misplaced amongst peers who don't match my game, I retire to my bed to find a new roommate who's half asleep on his side of the room. He awakens when I enter, and like most addicts recently recovering from their festering bullet wounds, we polish up our war stories and mix and match the ill-fated decisions where they've led us to - right here and now. He had recently overdosed on heroin and collapsed in an awkward position, perhaps imitating a pretzel, cutting the supply of blood to his legs. This rendered him a pair of crutches and without the use of feeling much of anything below his pelvis. Soft-spoken and polite in his mannerisms, I've never quite felt so much sympathy for an individual who seemed to have had his world utterly shattered to unretrievable bits due to a blinding addiction .. that is, until he made the choice to travel here and put in the work.

This forces me to wrestle with my thoughts on the power of addiction versus the invaluable (and consequential) importance of choice. Why are two men in their mid-20s, who've been given another chance at life, sitting at the ends of their beds in an exquisite rehab facility, lamenting the past choices they've made? Should we have not learned the first few times of embarking down the rugged roads of debauchery and should be forced to pay the ultimate price of consequence? Are we too socially spoiled to be granted access to areas such as these? Though some are forking over their own finances (myself included) to be here, some have the grace of government or perks of work to fund their stays. Have we come so far as a species that these group sessions, the unforgivingly over-the-top facilitated efforts of therapy following us around 24/7, are the only ways to get to the root cause of our near-suicidal activities? Why is it that when some require a hug, others require a smack? Our traits as beings stuck in our grave choices are all assembled by different ethereal hands. The alteration of brain chemistry on an unrelenting warpath takes place via the first initial choice to partake in it. Once choice plays out, the most authentic, most stark disembodiment of the soul will take place, and THAT is the very essence of the addiction being and becoming a *disease*. In order to be able to commit to the action of reaching, your internal circuitry must process "free will" and make the grasp itself. Of course, there are a plethora of other razor-tipped branches off of the tree of choice that make it damn near impossible to individuals once stifled with. As someone who suffers from the problems of addiction, I feel my opinion on this should be taken with a feeling of pleasuring the appetite rather than making one feel ill. I have put in the overtime and have had my life's experience be fully formed and moulded via the ramifications of hedonistic behaviour.

Night number seven, a week of being dead sober, grants me the fruitful offerings of deeper sleep.

It's a bright enough Sunday sky outside, looking like secretive forest fires are ready to rear their ugly heads here in B.C. A special day of allowing visitors to chit chat at the end of the weekend, my parents have come to visit me from the mainland. Dozens of family members of each inpatient here are gathered outside. As my parents see me through the wide door glass at the front entrance, the moment my Mom lays eyes on me, I can see her start to cry. The emotional pain causes me to wince, but I keep my cool in front of everyone, mainly for her.

We sit on a picnic bench outside, surveying some of the pleasing bright gardens surrounding the building. I relay my discontent with this place and try pleading with them for understanding. They both agree that if I feel uncomfortable here, I can come home and regroup. Was this more of an enabling & protective stance from them, or is this where I'll best operate and reforge my life from here on out? I'll forever thank them and embrace gratitude for having this option to always fall back on. Though there are years of uneasy family history on their property, the countryside display and aroma of its nature somewhat resembles a bit of a freeing rehab aesthetic. Maybe I'll do this and expect better results (this doesn't even come close to happening).

My parents leave as the visitor's hours expire. I'm forced to partake in an extremely awkward game of group charades to end the night, another problematic brick wall of social activity I want nothing to do with. I wish I had pulled the card that said, *"Act out someone who has wasted a relatively large amount of his own money in less than eight days and packs his belongings the next morning, getting the flying fuck out of this mouse cage"*. I played that character well the following day.

At roughly 6 am the next morning, I awake and assemble my gear. With my belongings packed the previous night into my travel bags and backpack, I'm just about ready to march towards the front office when I'm interrupted by a staff member checking in on my roommate,

"You're not planning on leaving, are you?" questions the young staff member, looking like he'd just been shot by a bullet, trying to process my decision to leave.

"Try to stand in my way," I reply, "We can make this fucking colourful if need be."

It would take a 10-time world MMA champion to bring me down at this current moment. I'm absolutely sick to my stomach trying to be chartered around like an experiment, some kind of test dummy for analytics and documentation.

I walk past him, with my backpack around my shoulders, and directly to the reception area, where I tell the Staff of my decision to no longer stay here.

They place me in the Chapel room while I eagerly wait on the couch I was sleeping on a few nights ago, looking to be free of these wrongfully masked walls.

An older counsellor comes in and patiently tries to change my mind. I don't back down. I ask him to leave. Forty-five minutes pass, and another counsellor, this time a little younger, comes in and starts to try to convince me that I'm making a bad choice. This is where my tone shifts from irritated to on the tip of being pushed to violence. I have no clue why, upon request, I'm not allowed to just walk out without this whole song and dance. I imagine the management team flipping out in the backrooms, realizing their coercive and interrogative tactics are met with immoveable resistance.

Just when I think the concrete has melted free, Gwen appears through the door and hastily sits down, almost bumping right into me. I guess word travels fast through this small residence.

She's evidently upset about my choice to part ways, but I know she understands. Gwen relays some of the nightmare stories from her life and reminds me to try harder once I'm back in the outside world. She jots her phone number and a cute message on one of the back pages of a book I've brought with me (a book one of the counsellors told me they were on the edge of confiscating due to its nature of downplaying the effectiveness of the 12-steps). I promise her that I'll be in touch once I make it back home. This promise is kept. I don't say goodbye to anyone else except for the two staff members at the door, nor do I even look back to survey any ounce of blooming, positive memories.

On the taxi ride to the Nanaimo airport, I turn my phone back on and deal with the influx of missed text messages and social media notification eruptions. It vibrates for a good two or three minutes of trying to manage the outpour of worried individuals. I double-checked my bank account and made sure the money I had deposited to the Rehab facility was placed back into my account, minus the days I stayed. It has been returned to its rightful owner.

The flight back to Calgary is riddled with bottomless thoughts. It is in the hands of the individual to want to make the change, to want to take their commitment to rehab as seriously as possible if they wish to harvest the benefits of a newly refurbished life style. Many people covered with the unwashable tattoos of addiction find solace and a new layer of skin in Rehab; it's just not for me. You have to be receptive and allow for the governing hands of trained psychotherapists, doctors, psychiatrists and other staff to help understand mental illness and addiction to bring you to a new frame of mind. Often, this only works for those who can drop their ego and their stubborn traits. I was not one of those people. I had not found the guiding beams of the lighthouse to direct my line of vision to the shore. I still cling to the lonesome buoy out in the ravenous Pacific. To those who find their way due to the provisions of Rehabilitation, I applaud you and welcome you back to sanity.

I trip up the *12 Steps*. Having failed enough times trying to adhere to them was stiff enough evidence to put down that book and begin to figure this one out on my own. You cannot be in a worse situation when some goof with blinders on is spouting off how successful they have been in their lives with it, how you're doing it wrong, and how they're doing it right. The Egotism in some recovery groups is baffling beyond comprehension.

To quote the late and great George Carlin, "The larger the group, the more toxic, the more of your beauty as an individual you have to surrender for the sake of group thought. You will do things in the name of a group that you would never do on your own."

Returning to Alberta, I'm able to stay sober for only three weeks before I make the concrete choice of moving back to B.C.

Alcohol follows me over the provincial line from Alberta to British Columbia.

With all of the windows fully down in my GMC Jimmy, the Summer winds on the highway through the Kootenays refurbish my vehicle's upholstery with sun-enriched natural lifeblood from the sky. The fourteen-hour drive home from Calgary to Abbotsford is spread out into three days. The first night, I pull off into the city of Cranbrook, having a few glasses of wine with a fancy gourmet pasta dish, the proper way wine is supposed to be consumed. It doesn't create a stampede of horned bulls to overthrow my life like I would have usually thought would take place. I'm able to put a cork in the drinking as soon as I'm finished with dinner. The same goes for the following night, parking in the city of Princeton, where I hit up a local pub and have another few rounds of Merlot paired with a mouth-watering steak dish. Again, I don't drink anymore once I return to my hotel room.

It's only when I get back to my hometown of Abbotsford that it's time to swallow liquid forms of dynamite and hope for the best. Returning back to my parents for barely 45 minutes to say

"Hello," I call Mitch to meet me at one of our old watering holes, Abbey Tap House, where we nearly OD on Witbiers and Ales. We're clearly excited to see each other after not seeing one another for six months. A few other friends join us in the process, most of them gazing upon me, dumbfounded beyond comprehension to know I've just gotten out of rehab and am already back to my old self, consuming Alcohol like a madman. Nobody really says anything. I don't say anything about it either. The kid at the back of the class with his headphones on for the entire lecture; I've learnt absolutely fuck all. This last month, which has granted me the chance to finally get it right, has left me $12,000 poorer and brings me back to the sickness of juggling my vital organs around in my hands for the world to watch.

Three years of the same antics will pass, riddled with brief periods of no Alcohol followed by an all-you-can-drink Niagra Falls fluid capacity charged with booze sort of bender. I revisit Rehab for the second time in August of 2019, lasting for 22 days in the city of New Westminister. I waste another $9,000 to rule out the option of Rehab ever working for me. I leave three weeks in due to the pitiful concordance of how the counsellors interact with clients. I labelled it the *School of Hard Jocks*, overrun with hot air balloon-sized egos and boulder-headed machismo clownery. There are a few good people I'll meet in there, some that I've known through other friends for years, but in the confines of closed walls and closed minds, it will never work for me. Period.

From 2021 to 2022, I'll be able to stay sober for an entire year, solely for the purpose of impressing my girlfriend, Valerie, and revelling in the attention from dopamine hits via small heart icons from Facebook and Instagram likes. The accumulated 365 days of sobriety was a reminder to never undergo such a vivid life transformation if it's not done for the love of and for yourself. Nobody else can bring you to fresh air unless guided by your own energetic weaving. Nearing the end of my year-long cleanliness, I will spend the next 10 months relapsing, slowly crawling into a wood chipper and becoming trapped in the filthiest of alcoholic suffocations. Marked with immeasurable loss and introduced to the final boss, Death, the two of us swing-dance in a celebration in a pitch-black concert hall, twirling and whirling to its own everlasting supremacy.

CHAPTER 7

La Nuit où j'ai perdu Mon Copilote

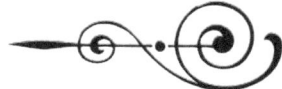

June 2022
Lake Country, B.C., Canada

I've just voluntarily released myself from the Kelowna General Hospital after drinking close to a litre of Rum a day for ten days. They want to keep me for longer, but I decline, knowing there is nothing more emotionally degrading than lying in a hospital bed while listening to the carnage of neurosis and death exhibiting its sounds of torment all around. That IV needle is torn out of my flesh the moment I feel I can walk a straight line again. When the bubbles of my thoughts begin to float higher without bursting so quickly & violently - it's time to go.

Nearing the end of this bender, I was pulling chunks of black & red esophagal matter out of my mouth with already plasma-soaked hands. Visions of the nights that had passed before this bring back face-ripping regret. I slightly remember being back at my house in Lake Country, shoving one of my closest friends, Javon, across the kitchen table as he came over to see if I was okay. My girlfriend, Valerie, had made a call/cry for help to any of my friends close by, and he answered it. I treated him by almost ejecting him through the door of my house. A brief image of him pouring out my rum in the Kitchen sink returns to my memory bank. My violent outburst makes more sense to me. That's something you do not do to a struggling Alcoholic who is in the throes of addiction. Though it was slowly killing me, at the same time, what he was pouring down the sink was the substance that was quite possibly keeping me alive or saving me from the extreme complications of withdrawal. Javon didn't understand this, nor did Valerie. I can't blame them. Echoes of Val's disgruntled voice, paired with fear, join this acidic web of loathing and embarrassment of myself. Closer to the end of this horrendous, almost two-week-long exhibit of displeasure, my vomit resembled oozing blackberry jam that was being mixed with half-solidified concrete. Each time I was hurling pounds of stomach juices into the porcelain bowl, I was convinced they would be my final breaths. There's no room for air when your lungs are empty - you go to refill them, but you're still projectile vomiting. Over and over. This is how many people will die from Alcoholism, usually in their sleep. The act of self-care has jumped off a thick branch from the Tree of Sanity, swinging high above the ground from the Hangman's Noose. During all this, Valerie calls me an Ambulance to bring me to safety. I don't want to leave my house, but the bewildering thoughts of trying to tough this out start to embrace the impossible. Before the medics arrive, I'm left to try and stabilize my breathing on the bathroom floor. I look up and see our Dog blinking slowly at me with concern. At this moment, I'm aware that most Animals can sense Human suffering. I want to kiss her softly on the forehead and remind her this will pass. Thoughts of emotional relativity are scorched to dust as the reek of vomit & blood nearly makes me want to break my own neck to end having to deal with this anymore.

After spending a day or two in the hospital, my first stop in the morning was to hit the liquor store. I'm aware I should refrain from purchasing alcohol after what I just went through. I'm aware of the extent of damage I take on every time this happens. However, I need it. I've become addicted to the feeling of this facilitating fury. A hurricane of embarrassing misery encompasses me for a brief moment. It fades when I must continue toward a fix.

Today, I'm not too fond of the way things have transpired. I have to return to my house in Lake Country, where Val is waiting. She gravely told me not to return or else she would bring the Police to our door. Perhaps I could use the Police to my advantage to rework this situation. Having them present could sway in my favour. I can get there early enough to apologize one last time & expect a warm caress of affection & understanding. After thinking this through, I phoned the Non-Emergency Police line and asked them to send assistance to our house. I explained my situation to them, and they agreed.

This might just work.

I couldn't have been more wrong.

I was taken via Ambulance to this hospital a few nights ago, rendering me without a vehicle. Still feeling a little woozy from what was given to me at the Hospital, I find a liquor store nearby and grab a six-pack of Heineken, storing them in a white grocery bag. I spend the next 30 minutes drinking three of them while resting against the back of the store. The other three are saved for later. I've got just enough money to get a taxi from Kelowna to Lake Country. It's a forgivingly brisk June morning. The last few violent days are scrambled and ejected out of my mind's atmosphere.

The red taxi meter inside this car flickers and rises like my recently recovered heartbeat. 23kms from the Hospital to my house. Seldom am I ever sober riding a taxi. I guess at this moment, I wouldn't be classified as sober due to the beers I have just slammed, but even those three beers have barely made a noticeable dent in my boomeranging anxiety. I say nothing to the driver for the entire trip. The stack of silence becomes a teetering tower about to come crashing into the dirt.

As we turn the corner into my neighbourhood and ascend the steep hill that is my driveway, I see that Val's car is parked outside. My car is still parked beside hers. I notice my right rear tire is entirely flat. Upon closer look, the rim is broken, too. I have no recollection of this happening, but perhaps I smashed into something (or someone) on one of my liquor store runs. I notice a light on in our dining room. She's home. I can't even remember if I paid the Taxi driver as I exited the cab. The tidal waves of anxiety offer many stiff elbows to my thought processes.

As I try to enter our suite, I see the locks have noticeably been changed. My key enters the door but fails to turn. Like when you've pulled all the muscles in your neck and are trying to look to the right or the left; it just doesn't happen. The intent is there, but there is no movement. I try our passcode - the luminescent padlock flashes red. Again. Again. I succumb to the realization of defeat. Valerie had changed the locks & passcode to get into our house. She contacted the landlord and had it done when I was in the hospital. In visible frustration, I quietly let out a barrage of curse words. As this happens, I look to my left and see Valerie standing in the window with our Dog & Cat by her side. Her eyes are dark & sombre. There is minimal emotion whirling about her existing aura. She stares at me like I've been dead in her eyes for months (which I have). As I place my hand on the window, I feel like hurling up the rest of the air in my body. Dry heaving whatever is left in my stomach after a week of draining fluids due to the unforgiving nature of binging on ethanol.

My memory bank falls back to the previous year of a road trip we embarked on to an area located in the West Kootenays of British Columbia: Whatshan Lake. The emerald crystalline and anti-human population surroundings of the gathered forests were a magnetizing birdsong for both our souls. We had already been together for about nine months. On the three-hour drive to get there, we visited a small swimming pool, engulfed with rainwater and barricaded by pine trees, tucked off to the side of the road called "The Hippy Hole". Being granted clear, clean cliffs and deep pools of water to plunge into, Valerie and I stripped down to our birthday suits and inhaled the intoxicating cedar-enriched air as deep as we could. Our adorable Cockerspaniel/Nova Scotian Duck Toller dog is with us, ecstatic and rummaging through the trees. Though Val chickened out from jumping off the thirty-five-foot ledge at the tips of our toes, I couldn't help but take the leap, roaring like a banshee, swearing violently on the way down, torpedoing into the luscious and cooling caverns below. The ineffable boost into livelihood with her by my side left an invisible tattoo on my skin that I still search for to this day.

After our escapades off the cliffs, we drive for another 45 minutes North, pulling off to a random clearing to set up camp. It's only Her, our dog, and I, with virtually no other Human life to be found for dozens of kilometres. Cellphone receptions are slaughtered, no electronic devices to alter our course, and only the curative hums of wildlife left to remind us that we weren't entirely alone. It borderlines misanthropy, but Val and I seem to connect better in terms of general distaste for humankind. She's able to rope me along with ventures outside my normal comfort zone of travel. My anxiety still spikes on travelling far without alcohol (as any lengthy trip in my early years was always undergone with a drink in hand), but with each passing month, Val shows me the beauty of getting out of the house without needing it.

The weekend was spent swimming, basking on the sunny & sandy deposits on the sides of the lake, clinking our non-alcoholic wine together, and going over the books we chose for the trip.

We sleep in the back trunk of my SUV-style Ford Escape, placing the seats down for both of us to cram together. Val, being 5'2, fits perfectly like a small Tetris block inside the space provided. I, being just under 6'4, barely have enough room to maneuver around without feeling like I'm being held in a hostage cell, but I get used to it. At night, when the temperature drops to a near-freeze, we use a small, tightly closed jar of hot water placed between us, under the blankets, to provide warmth as the night passes. It's a trick she showed me learned from her days of backpacking around the world.

Slivers of the windows are open to allow the night sounds to aid us into dreamland. Crickets conversate in the moonlight while Loons talk trash to each other across the vast stretch of lake water beside us. The nocturnal creatures provide us diurnal folk with the lullaby frequencies we need to secure a quality deep rest. The peace of a forest during the night in the Kootenays is next door to Heaven.

Of course, we do this trip 100% sober. The importance of the wine being non-alcoholic could not be more stressed. Val did her damned hardest to try and honour my sobriety by picking up non-alcoholic drinks throughout the course of our relationship. I knew she liked to sneak beers to herself here and there when I wasn't around (many times, I'd come over to her place and be able to taste beer on her lips, which she would just stress that her day was difficult and she tried her hardest not to drink before I came over but failed). She will never have to experience the decontamination of the senses as I have with booze, so I can't form anger about someone being able to control their drinking habits while I never could. I won't and cannot blame her for trying to do so, but investing in a long-term commitment while trying to uphold sobriety, with another being who still drinks Alcohol, will destabilize both of you in the end. I feel the potency of the *drunk love* I hold for her is far more potent than any other form of *drunk* I'll find in life. I deeply want to believe this is the truth. I am fatefully wrong.

I'm returned to the present, perceiving her figure through our living room window.

"Please," I quietly asked from outside of the window, my hand still on the glass, "I will try harder this time to make a change."

It's too late, far beyond the expiration date of something that has dug past the standard six-foot grave. This issue has fracked itself much lower to the intestinal ends of Hell. Irretrievable, untraceable, and no longer containing elements of fusible emotion from one member of the pact. She morosely shakes her head. Everything I beg of her is denied and rejected. I feel like breaking the glass with one of the boulders on the ground outside of our place (though that would quickly usher me to a jail cell that I don't wish to lie down in). I don't want to scare her or cause any more discomfort, nor do I want to startle our Pets inside of the house. I'm thinking of an exit plan, but at the same time, I'm still wondering if more pleading could grant me entry. All of these thoughts combust into the tree sap scent around me as I notice a Police cruiser climbing up our driveway. They've answered my call.

Two officers slowly step out of the car. I'm standing locked out of my own house with everything I own packed into my two-door car. Val had taken the proper time to perfect her Tetris skills by tossing everything I owned into the trunk and onto its seats. I'm so overwhelmed by sorrow that I feel I could start sinking through the hill we are standing on. Sinking past the metre-wide roots of decade-old trees & weeds. Choking on oceans of dirt and having my vision severed by the needle-like pincers of thousands of insects galore.

No horseshoes. No four-leaf clovers for a remedy to misfortune. The pair of Police officers agree with Valerie that I have no say in this matter. She has taken the time to work with our Landlords, coming up with a newly crafted Tenant Form for this place, excluding my name from it. I now legally hold a miniature candle to this storm of juridical wind. All of my words are rotted compost. I'm no longer on the lease and am now standing here wondering if I'm now considered trespassing on this property.

Again, I look at her through the downstairs window. I've spent the last year and a half beside this woman, day and night. As I peer through the glass towards her, there's no doubt in my mind that I still love her. Tough, wholehearted, and headstrong, once she has made up her mind, there's nothing in the world one can do to alter it. I've allowed this entourage of characters brought on by my Alcoholism to destroy us. There is no blame game to be invoked on anyone else. If I were to point any fingers, the bones would be snapped backwards to aim towards myself.

Let us recognize this moment in time that is so cloaked in an ashen blanket and brought to the most vicious of accident scenes on a highway full of fender benders; I feel disgusting and ready to sign out.

I asked the Police officers once more if there was anything they could do. They confirmed there wasn't. Val's eyes followed me until I got into my car, where I could see her shut the blinds—

another sign of inefficient closure. Her presence quickly became a trailless vapour.

I kept a safe distance between myself and the Cops as I spoke with them. I wasn't sure if they could smell the beer on my breath. I even checked if the wind was blowing in the opposite direction so the scent could travel away from their nostrils. There's a guarantee that Valerie knows that I've already been drinking. Heavily biting my lip, I fear she may blurt something through the window to the officers. Thankfully, she doesn't speak up. I'm sure she wants me off the property. With imaginary dumbbells channelling my spirits to a bottomless tomb, I get into my car and exhale like trying to blow out a thousand candles simultaneously. Cramped amongst a two-door Sedan, surrounded by the belongings I've accumulated after an entire year of cleanliness, the dripping waste of losing my grasp on sobriety squeezes my Lungs with gloves embroidered with titanium spikes. I'm unaware this feeling will be my closest ally for the following year.

With a cracked wheel rim, deflated tire and virtually nowhere to go, I begin to roll my car down the hill of the driveway, feeling each rock & micro divot in the path. Each full rotation of the broken wheel lathers the vicissitudes of current existence like darts thrown at my nerve endings. I make it to the bottom of the hill. The Officers follow my trajectory downwards. There's a small gas station at the end of this street with an air compressor that can refill this blown tire. I'm aware the rim is damaged, and this tire won't hold full PSI without causing a disturbance to safe & proper vehicle requirements. The Cops follow right behind me to the Gas Station, where I exit the car and try to add air to the tire.

"Are you going to be okay?" questions one of the officers.

In the most enormous heap of masked bullshit I've ever mustered in words, I reply, "Yes. I'll be fine."

Both Officers assessed the situation as "fine" and took off into the glowing warmth towards the South.

My options are handed to me like Doomsday Tarot cards reading ***"DEATH"*** for every pull from the deck. Do I return to my Parent's house dragging my sorry ass like a B-movie slasher does to his fresh kills back to the basement to dissect? Or do I muster the gallantry, duking it out solo for another test of crumbling wits? I choose the latter.

It takes me a few minutes to put on the spare tire in this parking lot, but through the soggy humidity, I manage to get it in place. These tires never fail to look hilariously ridiculous on all levels—they save the day.

After replenishing my regular quota of beers, I check myself into a hotel across town. I don't trust anyone or anything at the moment and don't risk leaving my belongings in my car. Tossing boxes and articles of clothing into my newly rented room gives me a swift blow to the gut of how minimalist I have always been. Aside from a few instruments, I tend not to hold on to much, which works great if having to move around.

I spend the night with my USB Keyboard plugged into my laptop, making soundtracks and song ideas based on my experiences from today. Here, I'll form together a piano piece titled "Our Final Auburn Sunset" bleeding out every emotion I can pay attention to while allowing the departure of Valerie to settle extreme unease into my veins.

Before I drift to bed, I watch highlights of the Stanley Cup Finals on TV. I reminisce about 11 years ago when I was 19, fading into sleep while remembering a hectic time of tumultuous anarchy and rioting psychosis.

CHAPTER 8

Sanctimonious Rioting and Embracing the Flashbangs

<u>Mid-June 2011</u>
<u>NHL Stanley Cup Finals</u>
<u>Downtown Vancouver, B.C., Canada</u>

I'm in the passenger seat of my Dad's Ford F-150, barrelling towards Vancouver's literal rumbling/crumbling downtown core. It's hosting Game 7 (the last game) of the Stanley Cup Finals. The Vancouver Canucks have brought the Boston Bruins to a do-or-die competition of strength, hockey wits, talent and skill. The amount of jampacked anticipations, frustrations and amalgamations that have been formed for this matchup is next-level pandemonium. I've been an avid Canucks fan since the age of six (going to my first game in Grade One with my Father), but these last few years, getting to meet more fans as I age skyrockets my interest in the team. Their lineup for this Playoff run is pretty god damn stellar, to boot.

Though my boss is a poorly trained, pea-brained, condescending asshole, he allows me to leave work an hour early to get from Abbotsford to Vancouver (usually a one-hour drive) to be a part of this monumental moment in our city's history. I would have walked out the door regardless of what he had permitted.

I prepped for this day by buying a 2'6 of Crown Royal whisky the night before. This morning, I hid it in my backpack at work. The temptation to prepare for tonight's matchup almost had me drinking it on shift.

On the drive in, I drink half of a one-litre of Coke, pouring half of the 2'6 of whisky in the Coke bottle, creating a gag-worthy potent half-and-half combo of pop and booze. During this, my Dad reminds me to keep the bottles below the window so no one can see the open liquor in the vehicle. It's been two weeks since I almost killed myself in my car accident, losing my license from drinking and driving, so I figured I'd have someone else do the steering for me.

We decided to stop halfway in the city of Surrey to take a Skytrain towards the boiling epicentre of Vancouver. There is no chance in hell we will ever get close to any of the heat if we dumbly try to drive in on our own. We know the Skytrain system. It will drop us off directly into the heart of the chaos. Every highway, sideroad, different route, or surface that could hold vehicles heading towards the city is gridlocked. Never in my life have I ever seen the amount of traffic like tonight. As ecstatic and ferocious as we all are in our frenzied *Sports Junkie* minds, I get a sense of gloom/doom when I see how chaotic life would become if some sort of apocalypse happened. These blocked roads cause tempers to flood the senses and spawn idiotic decisions. My Dad is the most famous in the family for losing his mind behind the wheel. He founded and created the most faithful, most rampant forms of Roadrage ever to have been documented. I'm a little nervous about him creating a scene for this trip toward tonight's attraction, but he keeps surprisingly level-headed. He's as excited as I am. Nothing is going to ruin our adventure.

The last I hear on the radio is that the Bruins have scored, and it's 1-0.

We're a few blocks from the Skytrain station, with not a single parking spot in sight. It's a commotion of people panicking, wanting to get downtown as quickly as possible. People are illegally parked and scattered across parking lots, no-go areas, and reserved spaces—the whole works. As we scrambled to find any possible parking area, I noticed one of my old high school buddies, Christian, walking past us on the sidewalk. We weren't entirely closely knit, but we had partied before, which creates a *bro code* between two individuals. I yell at him out the window, "Hey, Buddy! What the fuck is going on? Are you trying to get downtown, too?"

He looks shocked to see me slowly driving by. He yells back in agreement, also pursuing a night of shenanigans. We still have a few blocks to go, so I tell him to jump in the back of the trunk. My Dad laughs and agrees we could help him get closer to the train station. He hops in the back, laying low so no Police officers would notice. I give him a drink of whisky through the back window. By some divine miracle poured out of the Stanley Cup itself, we find a small parking spot that we spend milliseconds analyzing - we just need to get on that Skytrain and move towards the game.

This train station, which usually hosts a light amount of traffic on any regular mid-week afternoon, is now a bombardment of limbs and drunken maniacs. Onboard the railed domiciles speeding toward the city are an untamed, endless flow of hammered sports fans, obnoxious hometown critics, and an all-you-can-eat buffet of deafening screams and shrieks of Hockey hysteria. My Dad, Christian and I barely have room to jam ourselves onto the train. I just have enough room to raise my bottle of whisky & coke to my mouth. I pass some to my Dad to transfer the de-stressor effects of the alcohol to make this situation livable. One swig of this Crown & Coke is like a 60-minute deep breathing yoga session (without the sore limbs and manifesting of good intentions).

We made it to the downtown centre after a 15-minute advancement of hooting, hollering and hounding the whisky bottle. The moment we exited the Skytrain, we were blasted in the face with the breath of over 200,000 drunk and loony Hockey fans (us included). The pre-summer heat has already poured in off of the Ocean and circled between the street signs & jungle of buildings all around.

People are already getting arrested around me. Some were in handcuffs; others visibly wasted out of their minds, leaning against street walls. A definitive outcome for thousands as the night progressed. Thousands. Tens of Thousands. Hundreds of Thousands of Hometown jerseys and flailing lunatics stir about in this melting pot of alcoholic goons. Not all of the fans down here look or act like they'd be on "Canada's Most Wanted" list, but the majority are your average brute. The three of us stick close together as we march towards Robson & Granville Street. The city's massive fan zone section has a 100×100 foot Projection TV set up in the middle of the street. I don't know its precise size, but it's monstrous.

As we waded through the pouring flow of bodies, I ended up reconciling with my cousins, who had already been down here drinking for a few hours. My one cousin, Callum, who in many ways is the younger brother I never had, is well underage to be consuming booze, being just 16 years old, but not a single person gives a shit in such a warzone-like atmosphere. When the two of us get together, sheer and unadulterated chaos always ensues.

My friend Christian takes off into the crowd to find other friends.

We're too far away from the screen, so we find a restaurant to crowd into. The hockey game is deep into the second period already, and the Canuck's are down 3-0. You can feel the tension in the air, like scissors opening and closing near your eardrums. For some reason, my Dad takes off to find a different pub to drink at. Maybe he's tired of being around us drunken imbeciles and wants to lay low somewhere else. I say I'll text him when we're done here. I think he went to meet one of his old friends. It doesn't matter what generation you were a part of - this is a critical moment in all our lives as Canucks fans. Whether you were born in the '50s or '60s or were around for their previous Stanley Cup run in 1994, we're all in this together.

Callum and I are pressed to the sides of a wall, trying to get a glimpse of the TVs mounted on the wall of the bar where we're struggling to get a seat. Every square inch of every pub in Vancouver is brimming past the full line. We notice a table with two older women that has two empty seats. Without a second of questioning, we both flail over and park our asses down on the wooden chairs. We don't even have to introduce ourselves when one of the older ladies flat-out offers us to drink from their pitchers of beer. Their generosity throws a brick right into the face of sobriety. This sets the course of our sails down an obstacle course full of tipsiness and maniacal hooliganism. I must have drank 2 to 3 pints in a matter of minutes. Callum is also drinking as much as possible. While we were doing this, I was able to order a massive pitcher of alcohol-filled Long Island Iced Tea. I've never liked this particular drink, but it was the first thing I saw on the Menu. It's often a drink that's higher in ethanol percentage. I hastily tell our server to bring it as fast as they can.

From how close the Canucks are coming to elimination, let's loose a Nuclear Bomb explosion of anxiety from the downtown centre of Vancouver to all the other areas of the Province. Can they return from this 3-0 deficit with one period remaining? Callum and I eye the TV with uncertainty. It's at this point there's a paradigm shift surrounding our pursuits of the night. The only task at hand is to get now as drunk as humanly possible. We honour the Liquor Gods and drink to the good, bad, and the destruction of responsibility. The taste of the airwaves is an extroverted orgasmic dream world. I don't remember paying for the bill. In preparation for the forthcoming insanity, we set the tone right by making a break for the streets outside. There are way too many bodies surrounding us, and the amount of overcrowding is the perfect cover to get away with a dine & dash.

We weave our way towards the city's centermost heated area, Robson Street, where nearly 100,000 people are crammed into a *fan zone* square to get closer to the moon-sized television. There's a puzzling feeling of rage, confusion and drunkenness all around. I trip over dozens of intoxicated people sitting/lying on the concrete. I've lost count of how many girls I see passed out drunk with their boyfriends, trying to bring them back to reality. Every 50 or so people I pass by, someone is throwing up on the ground or ultimately passed out cold from alcohol consumption. It's a complete shit show, and nothing is about to get any better for those down here.

Eventually, we make it to this gigantic display of loss. Vancouver is now trailing 4-0, and the final few minutes of the game are playing out. Everybody in the crowd is swearing and starting to whip/slingshot things at the TV. Boos turn into profane assaults of colourful expletives. Liquor bottles explode against the screen. An assortment of half-full cans of beer and alcohol canisters come hailing down like a five-minute waterfall from the sky. Artillery is being launched from all angles of the city. I started to think we should be wearing helmets to avoid getting cracked in the skull with a glass bottle. I dodge a few of them.

In one of the only acts of violence that I'll commit throughout this night, I grab a plastic water bottle and whip it at the screen (this was caught on a YouTube video and can be found if searching for the final moments of the hockey game's duration coming to an end). I know this is just a game, for god's sake, but the investment of emotion into this year's Stanley Cup run weighs on the *good guy* conscience of the brain & soul.

The end of the game nears with just a dozen seconds left in the third period. As the hourglass runs dry, the city becomes wet. Wet with inebriation and a testosterone-fuelled disorder. Demented and without any form of rationality. I am a drunk 19-year-old being emotionally lit to the heavens with curious valour and excitement, encapsulated in this massive party, investigating the ongoing brutality and where it'll take me. The zero on the clock hits. The game is over, and people lose their fucking minds. I look up and start screaming. Callum and I are right below the gargantuan television set. To my right is a famous CBC reporter who gives me a severely freakish look. Hundreds of goons are screaming, "RIOT! RIOT! RIOT!" and "FUCK BOSTON! FUCK BOSTON!"

We're now dispersed into a tide of caveman-like mental defects yelling at the sky, cursing god, and taking their frustrations out on the city around them, reduced to the primitive functions of smash & rage.

I notice a massive plume of smoke down the street from us. I tell Callum we should go figure out what's going on. Like mosquitoes to a blinding lamp, we follow the crowd and try to decipher the smoke signal.

The closer we get, the more shit starts being sent into a planetary fan. Fights are breaking out left and right. Unassociated randoms begin smashing the windows of every business up and down the streets of Northwest Downtown Vancouver. The looters begin their frenzy of snatching valuables and flashy items. Very few want to play the heroes of protecting the city, while many more wish to bring this place to smouldering ruins. Men are running on top of Porta Potties, which have been set up around the city. I see a guy fall through one of them and come crashing through the door, spraying feces and piss into the air.

Toilet paper is dragged around an entire city block, with cops scrambling to close certain intersections to keep crowds at bay. For every one police officer, there are about 100 unhinged rioters.

A few blocks away from us, due to many people retreating from the violence, we heard there was a drunken army of mobsters flipping civilian and police cars over. This explains all of the dark smoke and explosions happening north of us. Some weren't rioting (Callum & I included). Still, it was just as bad for them to be there watching and giving these animals the adrenaline to feed off of (due to the increasing popularity of Smartphones and vigilante reporters around this time, this would help criminal investigators and the RCMP find those responsible for the worst of damages held accountable, handing out criminal sentences and hefty fines). I'm able to capture a few videos with my cellphone, perfectly capturing the mentality of an endless lot of lost souls here with me. From afar, I'm filming a teenager smashing a store window with a small crowbar, only to be tackled right out of his shoes and have his face broken into the concrete. Nobody knows what to do. And this is primarily because of our best friend, Alcohol. The game has long been over. The rational mind would suck up the loss and head home in hopes of a better tomorrow, but that's never going to happen with Alcohol calling the shots, all of it frothing in our bloodstream. The odds of how severe this all becomes would cease to exist if it weren't for binge drinking, the requirement of booze to always be associated with this sport, and our Canadian Culture being so bloody obsessed with having to lather any time past 4 pm with suds and liquor. It's a cultural phenomenon that will end up costing many a grave debt due to the conniving lacerations it forever applies to the human spirit.

We mix and mingle with an array of different chaotic guerillas of the night, sometimes fist-bumping and screaming, "FUCK BOSTON!" together, or sometimes getting in shoving matches, often being forgotten about in a few seconds. We all retain the memories of a goldfish, seeing things exploding, breaking, collapsing, and then moving on to the following article of extermination. The carnage is becoming incalculable. As we hear people, side shops and cars being beaten to a glass-shattering pulp, I look up and witness a street sign go flying in a zigzag motion and nearly decapitate a woman a few metres ahead of us. She goes down like an anvil in a pillowcase. Her boyfriend whips his head around, looking for the son of a bitch who threw it. No one can predict these projectiles or where they're coming from.

Much like the game of hockey, you have to keep your head up, or you're going to get decimated. More malicious minutes pass. I come close to a severe physical altercation. I found a two-litre of Coke on the ground, figuring it would be a good idea to open the cap and toss it into a crowd of limitless people. The spray of the pop foam douses two burly Men standing ahead of me to my right. These goons look straight out of an Eastern mafia movie. They glare back at me, with frowns stretching to their feet as if they're about to pounce on my Cousin and me, shanking us with whatever sharp object they have concealed. I profusely apologize and grab Callum by the shirt, running off in the other direction. I give them the finger as we disappear into the next zone.

I have my phone in front of me at all times, trying to videotape the ever-evolving carnage. In a gut-busting event to coat this experience with more laughter than violence, I pretend to be a "famous news reporter" who works for a Canadian Media outlet. Callum and I walk between people, holding my cell phone like a microphone, and ask them their thoughts on this situation. Some folks believe me, going off on emotion-filled attacks on how pathetic the people of this city are, while others look at me like I'm the biggest fucking clown on the block. While doing this, some idiot runs by and tries grabbing my phone. He fails and runs off down an alleyway. This is a time when you'd hope you have zippers in your pockets due to looters and pickpocketers running about.

The Ape mentality continues. Someone standing on the sidelines is randomly sucker punched and collapses to the ground, kissing the concrete. It reminds me of a real snuff video of when someone is shot in the head. The way their body drops is nauseating. Gravity pulls their skeleton downward as if they're made of rubber.

The night is becoming pretty nasty. I videotape a tough guy trying to protect a sheet of glass outside of an insurance claim business. He and a few others are doing their best to wear

Superman capes, drunkenly defending something for their own powerful ego. It makes no sense to play the Hero in this psychotic safari. A group of other guys are berating them, trying their best to break the plate of glass. The men protecting the store are able to keep them off. One of the thugs in the offensive group mouths, "I will find you." The defending tough guy replies, "Try finding me, you fucking goof!" (A day later, this tough guy was interviewed on the news with a huge bandage over his chest. I am going to assume the group of other men did find him and stabbed him. He's lucky to have kept his life that night.) A guy to my right is so intoxicated that he fumbles with the brick he's carrying and just falls over. The sight is so hilarious and saddening at the same time. I'm not sure how, but we bump into my friend, Christian, again. The chances of colliding with him are about 1 in 100,000 due to this ocean of goonery, but it happens. He sticks around for a bit and then vanishes. I even smash shoulders with one of the Dads of another old high school friend. Even though my hometown is about 100km east of where we're at right now, there appear to be quite a few familiar faces in this delirious dilemma. I get a video of us screaming together. He drunkenly yells my nickname out loud, "JORDO!!!!!" and stumbles away. We're all beyond maxed out on our idiot level.

We've been down here for over an hour, aimlessly parading through the static and chaos addicts. I've been keeping my Dad updated on where I'm at. Without warning, he manages to find us in the crowd.

"Callum and Jordan," he expresses in graven fear, "Let's get the fuck out of here!"

The moment he finishes his words, someone tosses a small statue through a bank window right beside us. People are defacing some of the walls with graffiti, and hockey sticks are being thrown all around.

Callum and I are having too much fun, fuelled like out-of-control missiles being drawn towards the heat. Like kids trying to be escorted out of the ballroom playpen by a commandeering parent, we ignore my Dad's call to safety and run off in the opposite direction, down an alleyway that connects to another street. There are too many bodies to give our positions away. I feel a slight wave of shame to abandon my Dad in this festival of emotional fireworks, but I'm aware he will make it back just fine on his own.

At this point, I really have no idea of where the night will take my Cousin and me. We're ducking between street signs, jumping over pylons and destroyed memorabilia, hopping over barricades where cars have been smashed into - it's all out lunacy, and we're loving every second of it. There's zero planning. We just gallantly run wherever the noise is the loudest. I look down at my phone and notice none of my texts or data is filtering through. I will learn later that the RCMP initiated the use of cellphone jammers to suppress the violence, not allowing others to reach out to their friends to join the madness. Callum and I come to a rest near a flaming garbage bin (not just a small can, but one of those large crates that garbage trucks require hydraulic forks to lift). Two men, one wearing a kilt and the other decked out in Canucks gear, are screaming for us to not walk in this direction. They aren't

Police Officers, so we just ignore them. I capture a few more videos of this incinerating metal and screaming bystanders.

Since we had travelled across a few streets connected by alleyways, there were a few (brave) stores with their open signs still lit up. We sit down in a Sushi bar to collect our thoughts, watching this urban massacre unfold on one of the televisions beside us.

What we're watching takes place on live TV and is no more than a hundred metres from where we're sitting. We make a few calls with the restaurant phone to our parents and assure them that we're just fine. Our words do little to bring forth calm to their lives, but it's the best we can manage. It's been a few hours since we've crushed any beers, so I ordered the largest can of Asahi, a Japanese Beer, that's on the menu. Here, I'll be reminded of my concrete drive to always have to keep alcohol with me when the going gets tough. The waitress eyes us both up and down. We look like toddlers. I get ID'ed. I show her. Luckily, I haven't lost my wallet in all of this. She reminds me that my cousin is not to drink anything. As soon as she walks away, I let him have some beer. We finish two large bottles, settle the bill, and make a run towards the still furious riots down the road, towards the eradication of decency.

We follow a group of a few hundred or so delinquents. It hasn't sunk in that we have no possible way of getting home or anywhere to stay. I imagine my Dad has already found his way back to the truck, heading back to Abbotsford. We're two teenagers ricocheting ourselves off the soundwaves of ruin. Neither of us has enough money to get a hotel room. It's closing in on 11 pm. We start to scope out a plan to sleep in an alleyway behind a dumpster. The thought of trying to rest near piss pools and a concrete swamp of vomit and rats at night is disgusting and scarily sobering (but not too sobering, as the whole point of this night is to stay drunk).

Before we can mould a plan into action, a solid line of riot police flood the area and disperse their tactics against the crowd. The rattle of their batons against the fortified riot shields they are carrying strikes fear into most of the bystanders. Callum and I make a bolt across the street. A mysterious clanking noise swims across the concrete; flashbangs are sent off just a few dozen feet from us. A girl in front of us drops like she was crushed by an invisible fist from the sky. Thinking back to playing any type of Tom Clancy video game in my childhood, I figured the best way not to be affected would be to not look directly at such a device. I turned away towards a brick wall—a ghostly jet of smoke blankets the area as I opened my eyes to the commotion. Dozens of scoundrels are running about. I see Callum looking like he's unconscious but still maintaining his upright posture. Worried about his safety, I pick him up and carry him behind a concrete barrier. I can't tell if the Riot Squad were firing stun grenades or some other type of concussive-style weaponry. Fading off the radar from their sights, both of us lay low for a few minutes. Callum shakes off the encounter and seems back to normality (though none of this night has been anywhere near the definition of *normal*).

My phone begins rumbling out of its shell. A minimal amount of cellphone reception is granted back to the city.

Callum's oldest sister, my other cousin, Dominique, is staying at a hotel a few blocks from where we're hiding out. Though we are still gungho and dancing with the youthful zeal of being teenagers, both of us agree to retire our Jerseys and fall back to a safe zone.

On our way back, I'm still in awe of how desperate human beings need to smash glass when occupied with fury. This transparent solid is the most sought-after element that succumbs to our wrath. Is it the sound of its explosion or the glistening aura of it littered all around that makes it so beautiful? I have no clue. I make sure not to step in any of it as it is legitimately everywhere in our path to security.

We make it to the hotel room, meeting up with my other Cousin and all of her friends. Callum and I don't say much other than that the night has been exhilarating and fucking relentless. It's about 1 am. Almost entirely forgetting about the whole point of coming down to this event in the first place, we pay attention to the TV that's on in the main room and wince at the highlights of the actual game. The commotion of the riot seems to dominate the headlines more than the sport itself. Everybody in this charade of a barbaric mess deserves five-minute majors for roughing, fighting, slashing, high-sticking, and embellishment, plus a 30-game suspension handed out by the strong arm of the law. While we never partook in this anarchistic and idiotic overthrow of the city itself, we got sucked into the magnetizing draw of drunken terror entirely captained by our young and curious minds.

I thank my older cousin for letting us crash here. Callum sleeps on a small loveseat, looking uncomfortable as all hell. I take off my Jersey and use it as a pillow on the solid floor. When I think back on our idea to sleep outside, I realize that this is a luxury.

Battle-torn and like two soldiers who were dropped on their heads in training camp, Callum and I stumble out of the hotel room the following morning. Last night's adrenaline rush entirely paved the way for my mental strength to pulverize any ounce of a hangover possible. The city is comatose. If a city were able to be prescribed anti-depressants to bring it back to life, now would be that moment. Most roads are entirely shut down. I can still smell the booze emanating from the downtown core, but perhaps that's just from my unbrushed teeth. I stick out like a bleeding thumb, still wearing my Canucks jersey. I feel like a Sniper could be on any of the surrounding rooftops and take me out with a quick bullet. It feels disgraceful to wear this thing, but I know the real fans weren't to blame.

There's a large crowd gathered just across the street from us. The mayor of Vancouver is being filmed on live television, being grilled on why all that has taken place in the last 18 hours was able to happen as if the alcoholic consumption and innate structure of animalism in hooligans was all his fault. A part of me wants to run behind him, start doing breakdance moves, screaming, just doing the most ridiculous shit imaginable to be caught on television to really keep pushing how mindless all of this was. I tell Callum we should try this out. We both laugh our asses off and walk by, obviously holding back our childish excitement as we had already spent our weekly quota on it last night.

If pocket lint were a currency, then I'd be close to Royalty status. My body cringes as I check my bank account. The remaining chump change I have in my grasp forces me to take on a responsible role to try and get Callum home safely. There are no more dollars left to spend on juvenile derangement. We find a payphone on the wall and call our Moms. Again, they are not pleased with our choices. When each of us makes our calls, we look at each other and make faces like Jim Carrey would in Dumb and Dumber.

I learned my Dad had made it home safely last night. I imagined when he walked in the door without me, my Mom was most likely traumatized.

I get us on a Skytrain towards the Greyhound Bus station off of Main & First Avenue. When booking our bus tickets back to Abbotsford, I explained our situation to the attendant at the ticket station. She giggles and hands us our tickets, taking one last look at us, thinking, "You two are really fucking stupid." I understand her soundless facial gestures.

We fall into our bus seats and recollect our survival stories of last night with laughter and awe as we trudge eastbound on Highway 1. On the venture back to the homelands, I remind myself how braindead it is to become deeply entrenched in a competitive game and have it alter your interactions with one another. The Sport of Hockey is fantastic, far surpassing the other sports, forever holding the most entertaining and fast-paced action to unfold in front of watching eyes. However, the arm-to-chest pounding, baboon-flailing jackassery that comes with some of its elitist, premature IQ-leveled fanbase is downright painful.

Fast forward six and a half years; I'll be chartering to New York City in the middle of a blizzard to watch one of my favourite bands reunite for a final show. In this adventure, I'll take on the tough streets of Brooklyn, navigating downtown Manhatten blackout drunk, facing a new type of hockey crowd at Madison Square Garden, and dealing with the aftermath of a terrorist blowing themselves up with a pipebomb in mid-daylight.

CHAPTER 9

Torn Map

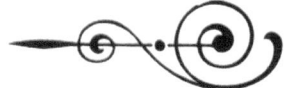

<u>**December 2017**</u>
<u>**New York City, United States of America**</u>

The rough and tough tumble of midflight turbulence reminds me of the days I used to be drumming for multiple Death Metal bands. The wings of this passenger airplane are like steel-plated drumsticks, doing blast beats (an aggressive drum beat) with the surrounding sky mist, rattling and rolling through the licorice black cloud juice. I could be 40,000 feet above North Dakota or Minnesota. I'm on a one-way flight to New York City (with no return date planned) to see one of my favourite bands, Moving Mountains, reunite and perform their last show. They're a combination of melancholic indie rock with sparks of hardcore & atmospheric ambient beauty (all of the magnets that pull me into a band that's not quite *metal*). I'm buzzed as all hell and feeling no pain. The extent of freedom is immeasurable. There's close to $50,000 in my bank account, a stiff swirl of Jack Daniels & Coke spinning around in the cup in my hand, and neither seat to my left and right is taken; space to lounge and be unchained from human interference. Does one drink in the Sky equal two on the ground? The math is so simple and graciously effective that it makes me chuckle aloud as I take advantage of this phenomenon, ordering another Jack & Coke, knowing I've confirmed my chances of doubling down on the booze.

Before the flight, I had around three or four strong beers on my drive to the airport (following up with a few more pints at the airport bar). The driving anxiety plays a ruinous role in trying to incapacitate me in my mid to late 20s. I will come to feel this for the next six years of my life, eventually having it mutate into a destabilizing phobia. Bustling around the bloated and cramped vehicular hysteria from my hometown of Matsqui to the Vancouver airport is enough to put any individual suffering from Amaxophobia (a fear of being on highways, in vehicles for too long; border lining Claustrophobia with a dash of Agoraphobia) in a concrete straightjacket. Every metre travelled is like trying to breathe as a swarm of Prehistoric Giants slowly but efficiently place truck-sized boulders on top of my body, one layer at a time. I may as well call this whole trip off, as this feeling is the deciding factor in so many inactions weighing my life down to its grave. However, every possibility is granted a defibrillating jolt back into coherence the minute I feel alcohol parade into my body. What was previously feared becomes a laughing stock and worthless mince-meat to the blades of my Ego. The concept of anxiety vanishes from my cognitive functioning. I'm ready to soar to the Moon, do cartwheels around its surface, dig to its core, host a rave, and party to the state of Nirvana, being soaked in its geysers of carefree ecstasy. Once the Ethanol has taken over, little can be done to bring me back home. Adrenaline is a helpful solider, often becoming the crutch that allows me to still walk straight even after a whole day of drinking. It is a hopeless paradox, making it possible for an aimless scoundrel to hit his desired bullseye. Being surrounded by such foreign sights on this adventure, this is the hormone that will conduct guidance for the duration of this trip. It becomes the scales of The Liquor Lady of Justice, allowing for a functional experience of a storm of GABA-inducing blitzkriegs and just a minimal plate of responsibility.

After the five-and-a-half-hour flight, I reach JFK Airport. I've collected all my belongings from Baggage Claims and headed outside to embrace the East Coast December Winter. Hailing a cab takes milliseconds due to the domino pattern of yellow & white taxis in unison outside. All of the New York license plates make me giddy. Nobody knows who I am. I don't have to worry about seeing anybody I may recognize. I get nothing but the finest of enjoyment out of this.

I booked a hotel close to the airport and hunkered down. The room is brand new but as small as an outback woodshed. The bed is basically 60% of the room. I take a mini bottle of rum and a can of coke out of the mini-fridge, which takes up 15% of the room, and mix it in the bathroom, which completes the rest of the 25% equation. I laugh at how small this unique box of a room is. I slam the drink and pass out in the marshmallow comfort of a freshly made King-sized bed.

I was able to remain sober for three weeks before this excursion. My mind has had enough proper sleep & weeks of recovery to make the morning withdrawals nonexistent. I know this is temporary. This is when my body begins to create its own military force, gaining thousands of soldiers & artillery each passing day. It takes roughly three to four days of heavy alcohol use to start to exhibit symptoms of agonizing withdrawal in the morning. Due to the extremity of alcohol abuse in my situation, each time I undergo the repetition of these patterns enables a neurological condition known as *Kindling*. The current literature on this highlights some staggering information about how damaging Binge Drinking and a consistent relapse, stop, go again, messes with neurobiological normality and creates behavioural malfunctioning. My only current defence is ignorance, and boy, does that cost me almost everything.

The following morning, I rise from the sheets, feeling relatively unscathed. Maybe I found the right equation of alcohol consumption that hasn't tattooed me with a *needing a wheelchair* kind of hangover the following morning. This room hasn't grown in size overnight. It's still as hilarious, dinky, and pipsqueak as it was the previous night. There's only one small empty bottle of rum from yesterday on the counter. I get a photographic wave of the unopened liquor bottles still in the mini-fridge. I'm foreshadowing my travels to get from this hotel to downtown Brooklyn. Maybe I should wait until I get down there and keep the drinking to a minimum until then? Fuck that. Why not chart out the next few hours with a drink from the Garden of Eden? The mini-fridge almost opens solely from the sheer force of my intentions. I whip together one of the strongest Screwdrivers known to Man. 99% alcohol—1% orange juice. The power of this drink may as well be considered Witchcraft. The spell it's put on me grasps like a recently sharpened bear trap. Now, with a fine-tuned engine due to the book of booze, I scratch the idea of taxiing down to Brooklyn and instead resort to travelling by Train & foot. I came this far to truly experience the aura of newly found authenticity.

Somehow, I time my departure perfectly and am able to catch a Hotel shuttle bus to a random Train station heading West. I purchased an International Cellphone Travel Plan to keep from being toyed with by Long-Distance Data overages, but that still doesn't keep my phone functioning correctly. The data circle spins as if I'm watching a wall of paint dry itself. I realize I'm left to fend for myself by being alert and noticing what sign points me to where.

Hopping out of the bus, the east core of Brooklyn levels me. Almost on cue, as my feet touch the ground out of the bus, police cars scream by. Firetrucks create small tremors in the ground around me. I notice far too many shady individuals rummaging to and fro, with litter playing tag with itself across the concrete.

The stereotypical downtown New York could not be more comical. The liveliness of all of this falls short, fast, as I realize how vulnerable I am out in the open. I've got an oversized backpack around my shoulders and am rolling my luggage to my side with all of my personal belongings inside. Lo and behold, the clueless

Canadian. Muggings and the threat of street altercations are uncommon back at home, but it feels like it would be all too scarily familiar around here. I should have just taken a taxi. I have 50K in the bank. For god's sake, I could have driven around in a fucking Limousine for this entire trip. Instead, I faced the noise. Nobody seems to mess with me. Perhaps my height & oversized winter jacket I'm wearing give me more of a threatening appearance, or maybe everyone is too high/drunk to care. Adding more pep in my step, I make it to a train station and board for the center of Brooklyn.

I exit the train as my phone's GPS finally starts to manage a few sparks of life. Vodka is still providing a small BIC Lighter amount of warmth in my veins. Immediately, I notice every Male looking as if they've been copied out of a book, thrown into a printer and multiplied by the hundreds if not thousands. This is the same for the Females. I've gotten off at a Jewish Ghetto and feeling incredibly out of place. Every Male, including most of the younger boys, is donning a solid black robe, a wide-brimmed hat, polished dress shoes and a bright white long-sleeved shirt. Their hair is left longer in certain sections, sometimes curled or shaved. Most, but not all, have tiny, circular glasses.

Here is a Canadian Male sporting a black toque, Converse shoes, a burly, deep blue plaid winter jacket and ripped black jeans, marching through a Jewish community with his belongings. The only thing I have in common with their outfit is the thick brown/black beard.

Block after block, I feel eyes slicing and dicing through to the deepest crevices of my soul. I have zero knowledge of this entire culture. I'm walking through the heart of it, feeling like picking up my luggage over my head and barrelling through while screaming just to escape this awkwardness. Fear aside, there is an odd wave of grandeur spinning around me. I hear school bells. Whiffs of crumbling winter leaves fill my nostrils. Schoolchildren trot by me, swivelling their heads 180 degrees to gawk at my exclusivity. This community doesn't make me entirely feel unsafe, but I have no clue if I'm going to be swarmed and shanked in a matter of seconds. I glance at my GPS map, which is now working correctly, and am almost out of the Ghettos.

I forge through a few more city blocks, taking in some stunning New York architecture. The searing cold of the approaching snow makes the layers of brick on the surrounding buildings brighter in hue. Branches of trees on the sidewalks are as bare as my efforts to remain sober throughout this trip. A drizzle in the ashen sky is cauterizing itself from a pearly white to a topaz gray.

After stopping into a random corner store to buy my first few gigantic American tallboys of beer, I've finally reached my destination outside of Williamsburg. It makes limited sense for me to have booked a stay at an International Hostel when I have tens of thousands of dollars readily available in my chequing account. I could have booked a suite at the top of a 5-star, exquisite, jewel-ridden pad - but that's just not me. The stay at the Hostel would be a great way to meet other travellers bouncing around the planet. I've stayed at hostels before, where the amount of partying was otherworldly. I wish to partake in the freedom of falling from great heights without a safety net.

I wear my Vancouver Canucks toque to show people I'm from another part of this continent (perhaps a tactic to be treated with more kindness). Because of its bright blue & green logo surrounding the Killer Whale (the Orca being the team's mascot), people notice it first, and the conversations stoke its tinders from there. Nobody this far East would be repping a Hockey team from the other end of the map, even if their family members were a part of it. Perhaps people fear some psychotic Hometeam fan is going to attack any Visitor repping other gear that doesn't resemble their own. While this thought spews into my mind, New York Rangers fans most likely remember the 2011 Stanley Cup Riots. They'll most likely leave me alone, remembering how unhinged and unpredictable a Vancouver Canucks Fan can be. I wear that with a badge of honour. Maybe they can feel it. Perhaps it's all bullshit. Either way - it works.

The hostel is reasonably well-kept compared to other rundown forty-year-old multi-layered shacks I've stayed in before. The lobby has a modern office style setting, while its halls are decked out with that vintage stone architecture I'll notice around the towns outside of New York City. There's a dimly lit games room on the main floor for people to mix & mingle. I imagine this is where most of the international social butterflies come to partake in exchanges and friendly banter. I'm not one of them. While the cost is often always correct, the discomfort of a hostel reigns supreme on too many levels to address. 95% of the time, you are paired with a host of other guests on military boot camp-style beds pressed against a wall. Dealing with the snoring of strangers rivals resting beside a chainsaw at full throttle. Grunts, groans and gross gurgles all about. Rarely is there a code of etiquette inside Hostels. I reminisce about my previous hostel experiences and quickly opt out of the shared room dilemmas, booking my own room (which most hostels don't often offer). While the bathrooms and showers are still shared, I'm pleased to spend a few extra bucks to have a closed-door & solo sleeping space. Again, I have no idea why I decided to set up camp at a Hostel when I have the funds to stay at higher-quality residences.

I make it to the third floor, find my room, and set my bags on the ground. There's a bunkbed on the wall and a small table to the side of it. That's it. The room is roughly ten feet long by ten feet wide. None of the walls connect to the roof so that sound can oscillate freely overhead from room to room, as per typical noise-ridden hostel structure. I figure I'll be so bloody drunk for this trip that none of the regular sleep disturbance anxieties will apply to me for the next few nights. There's an elongated mirror in which I snap a selfie. The distance from my Hometown to where I'm standing now is just under 5,000km. It's a rowdy experience, and the thrill makes me want to do a backflip off of the bed in excitement. The room is far too small for that, and I'd be sent through the walls from pulling off such acrobatics, so I try to settle down. I tuck my Canadian Passport into my backpack and slide it underneath the bed frame, hoping nobody finds my papered identity and takes off with it. Before leaving, I used the key they handed me at the front desk to lock my door and realized any clown could easily bust through these brittle defences. The thought evaporates as I head downstairs to face the streets of Brooklyn.

I refuel on quality American grease at some Burger joint I'm unfamiliar with. It's not a half-assed *the picture looks ten times juicier than the real thing* dilemma like Burger King, McDonald's, or A & W - this is your proper Yankee Doodle smackdown, cramming a quadruple pattie skyscraper of beef, amongst other delicious condiments. While taking it all in, I look up to survey the outside life. The streets and random folk remind me of Vancouver, but they've all been carved out a little edgier. Brooklyn would win in a UFC fight against Vancouver. Their character stats seem higher in strength, vitality and speed. Maybe not intelligence.

I hid one of the tall boys of Beer I bought earlier in my jacket. I crack one of them open at my table. I'm aware this is against the law, but nobody seems to care. Taking a risk this early into my trip to face the law is very moronic, especially as a foreigner so far from home. I do my best to keep it lowered, hidden beside me. I consume around 2,000 calories in one sitting. To this day, my metabolism works overtime and around the clock, 24 hours a day. Even after absurd nights of binging and taking in junk food en masse, my body figures a way to distribute it properly throughout the cells surrounding my frame. People often say how they wish they had the metabolic rate that I retain. That's a nice gesture and all, but this could also be working against me, as my liver joins this rate and processes Alcohol rather quickly, leaving me to scrounge for more and more.

I finish up my food and head towards the neighbourhood of Williamsburg to catch the band I've flown across the continent to see.

Williamsburg is filled to the brim with artistic hustle. Tucked across the bridge southeast of Lower Manhattan, I blend well with some of the surrounding crowd. I often dress like a Metalhead met a Hipster on a drunken night, and fornicated to the beats of sporadic death metal & indie rock. There's never quite a concrete aesthetic in my wardrobe. In places like this, it feels more comforting. I arrive far too early for the show, giving me time to survey the array of pulsation on this side of town. Architecture goes against the regular blueprint norms of design. Some apartments look like they're leaning far right or left as if they could topple over if there were an uneven weight distribution in one of the hallways. Vivid and blooming graffiti winds up the street lights and facades like poison ivy in a forest full of life. With time to kill, I find a random Bar I head into to continue poisoning myself.

It has always been a persistent struggle for me to try and meet somebody new without the use of alcohol feverishly running through me. Since the beginning of high school, I achingly battled with myself to be able to look someone in the eyes for longer than a few seconds. My drive to want to converse and stick around other folk was non-existent if a drink wasn't in my grasp. As a teenager and young adult, I'd flat-out refuse to go to parties if we were just drinking pop. I'd find myself overburdened with frustration if the night didn't consist of getting drunkenly unhinged, boringly staring into my plain jane drink, wishing for some kind of chaos to rise out of it. If the contents weren't brewing an uncontrollable armageddon from its alcoholic froth - I simply would not compute. Since the booze will be joining me for this whole ride, I shouldn't have a problem shaking some hands and getting to know some souls from the East Coast. Any place that serves Alcohol - I'm there. If this were a small barn with people sitting on broken hay bales, I'd find a way to get comfy. If this were a bleak crawlspace where you had to kneel down and sit on the freezing concrete, I'd work through it to maintain my buzzed levels of warmth.

After one or two Brookyln Winter Ales, I meet a couple around my age, Katie and Derek, from Washington DC, right off the bat. Sitting a few barstools down from me, I overheard one of them mention something about Moving Mountains, the band I'll be seeing tonight. I'm not really sure how to interject into their conversations, but I blurt out something creative: how unique the band's sound is on their latest album. I'm not quite belligerent drunk yet, but I'm feeling as smooth as a polished Jade stone. This gives me a few moments to bond with others over similar music tastes. I learned that both of them had been here for a few days and that Katie had been to British Columbia before, spending time in the Okanagan. How vast the seemingly endless vortex of the world can be is always immediately shrunken down to a pebble when you start making connections with strangers, realizing how miniature it truly is.

We gun a few more drinks, and I thankfully ordered and devoured a delicious steak dinner to try and absorb the number of beers I've had (and still plan to consume). We depart towards the Music Hall of Williamsburg. Though we go different ways once inside, I get their phone numbers in case they want to meet for drinks either tomorrow or the next.

Moving Mountain's performance brought whatever heaven is just a few metres closer to this Earth. My six-year obsession with the band is catered to my eyes and ears like the best orgasmic musical piñata eruption I could have asked for. The instruments are crisp but lukewarm, and their atmosphere floors me with a plethora of caged memories of my ex-girlfriend, Jes, from Illinois. Jes and I met using Instagram in 2013. Before the all-seeing gods of Algorithms took over what we first pay attention to on our Smartphones and when hashtags were more of a common occurrence to doomscroll through, one morning, I typed in *"#guitar"* and was shown an adorable, at the same time sexy, 20-year-old Mid-Western girl recording herself singing and playing with a beat up Acoustic on her bathroom floor. Back when our iPhones couldn't record without physically having to hold down the big red button on the front screen, Jes used one of her toes to hold down the filming button. Usually, I would pass by a video such as this, as if you've seen one, you've seen the next 100,000, but something taped my eyes firmly with construction tape, both vertically and horizontally, to keep watching. I messaged her right away. The two of us shared emails back and forth for months until finally adhering to wanting the physical connection, the intertwining of souls. Music kept both of us flourishing. The amount of baffling love we both had for Moving Mountains was a unique cohesion in our year-long relationship together.

As I watch the boys on stage belt out some of their best tracks, I call Jes, holding my phone in the air for her to hear. The call fails to go through. At this moment, she is a few states over to the West, beginning a new path with her soon-to-be husband. The ebb and flow of this familiar music brings me back to 2014 in Grayslake (Illinois), lying with her on her Father's boat, collecting every second of enriched, youthful romance for as long as we were possibly granted. A Midwestern momentous art piece, therapeutic & untradable, marvelling at our free Summer without restrictions except for the promise to be in each other's arms for its entirety. This is another reality where I considered starting a family with someone and allowed alcohol to viciously snap its neck. The feeling of illness has me disoriented.

I'm brought back to the wave of musical notes here in Williamsburg.

The hall floor is filled with headbobbing indie folk, all suited up with the latest and greatest in plaid and flannel designs. While I'm typically used to seeing Metal bands play live, with its off-the-wall sporadic nonsense on the ground level, maneuvering around what feels like a floor of active landmines, I'm glad there's no moshing for music such as this. I can enjoy the purity of emotion without having to keep my guard up 24/7.

Their performance goes on for just over an hour and a half. Wishing they would have stayed plugged in for the entire night, I fall back to the lobby.

After the room is cleared and the musicians have hung up their instruments to sleep, I notice the band members at their merch table talking with fans. I have no clue why, but I don't go up to greet and meet them like an ecstatic lifelong fan would. Instead, I head to the lower level of the venue and commit to what I've invested so much personal time towards: my Master's Degree of getting blackout drunk.

Like being wedged into a time machine that's malfunctioning, its rhythms and patterns fragmenting as each second passes, I awake as clueless as humanly possible. My eyes feel as if they've been staring into the dizzying blue flame of a blowtorch for the last hour. Maybe I was so out of it that I passed out with them open (which has happened in the past and scared the hell out of my friends). I've made it safely back to the hostel but have zero recollection of doing so. Who or what was guiding me? An angel just slightly less loopy than I was? I'm thousands of kilometres from home, a foreigner in an explosively busy & sleepless centre, and I was still able to hitch a taxi and manipulate myself around urban society. This perplexes me. How lucky am I to have managed to lose consciousness in New York City and return to my temporary home base without losing my life? The concept of luck chomps down on my throat. Buying a lottery ticket would make the most sense right now, but being a Canadian in America, even if I won, I wouldn't be able to legally cash it.

Assuming I'd have a stinger of a headache this morning, I saved myself some tallboys of beer in my backpack. I crack one open and drink it down; the headache fades. All my belongings are on top of the table to my left: wallet, phone, and travel bags. My Driver's license is on the floor, nearly broken in half. Clueless as to how it happened, I'm thankful that it's still intact and can be used as some form of identification (as I try not to haul my passport around, confined in the certainty that I'll lose it one trackless night).

It's late enough in the morning for some people to already be on their feet. I text the couple I met at the bar last night, Katie and Derek, to ask if they want to go out for morning drinks. One of them gets back to me surprisingly quickly, politely declining, and says they have to focus on getting back to their home state. They're probably wondering why the fuck I'm already asking to go out for drinks at 9 am. Nothing can or will hide my shame.

As I reach for my overflowing bosomy wallet, I notice it's crammed with dozens—possibly even close to a hundred one dollar bills. This sight triggers snippets of memories. I vaguely remember arguing with a bartender about the correct change for my tab. Instead of returning the money to my credit card, he gives me nearly eighty-eight one-dollar bills. I don't take the time to ponder why this occurred. If I were to sit with this wallet still tucked in my back pocket, I'd feel like George Costanza from Seinfeld, with his gargantuan leather case being lifted an inch higher when trying to sit down. I burst out laughing, having to stop myself, remembering there were other folk just beside my room still trying to sleep.

Enacting the typical scene of scanning through my phone while lying down, holding it with both hands out towards the ceiling, painfully hungover, I see that I've added some new friends on Facebook since yesterday. I recall meeting two hockey fans, Ryan and Giuseppe, at the venue's bar last night; both were around my age and excited about a New York Rangers game happening at Madison Square Garden tonight. I double-checked my bank account, and indeed, I see I purchased a lower bowl seat for the game at $300 USD (having used the Currency draining website of StubHub). With the flourishing amount of cash in my bank account, daily expenditures reaching $1000 mean very little to me, mainly pushed by an alcohol-doused manic rocket.

Gunning for some more excitement and running off a slight high from the beer freshly consumed, I gather myself together, run downstairs, and hit the closest bar outside of the hostel residence.

The moment I sit down, the bartender makes a comment about my Canucks toque. We shoot the shit back and forth, commenting on who has the stronger of accents. Who's more challenging to understand, that classic downtown Brooklyn troublemaker or the Great White North boneheaded Canadian punk? It's a friendly game of international fellowship that others in the bar take notice of and laugh at. I make a strong point to prove that Canadians can drink more brews than Americans could ever imagine. I tighten the boxing gloves around my liver and go in for the kill, consuming five double screwdrivers in under 30 or so minutes. The bartender, who looks impressed and concerned at the same time, settles my bill for the sake of my sanity. I appreciate the gesture and hit the streets to partake in the wanderlust through a New York blizzard. Thinking about the Hockey game tonight, I head back to my room. At least, I think I make it there.

The clock reads 6:15 pm on my phone and a starting time of 7:00 pm on my hockey tickets. I jolt up from my bed, not having a fucking clue where I'm at. This keeps happening. The blackouts are occurring earlier and earlier. I ignore it and scramble downstairs to catch a cab (which is not too hard to do here in New York). There's no reason to tell the driver to apply both feet to the accelerator, as he's well-trained in barrelling through traffic and looking at the yellow light as if it were still green. Why is there an option for that dreaded colour? It's Green or Red here - that's final. I internally gasp in silence as we cross the Brooklyn Bridge, and I bear witness to the World Trade Center building from afar. It's a looming totem figure making an outstretched yoga position towards the clouds. I travel back in time to 2001. Waking up on a school morning at 7 am was a rarity, but for some reason, I was drawn to my living room, hearing sounds of trauma coming out of the TV. My Mother was sitting on the couch with her hands over her face in fear of what was being displayed on television.

I clearly remember our old school 32" big boxed tele unveiling the live chaotic carnage while all else were forced to watch from a distance. The South Tower had just collapsed. What remained was what looked like an artillery-shelled city with one lacerated skyscraper remaining. The World Trade Center was brought to my attention a year prior, watching an episode of The Simpsons where Homer ascended to the top of one of the towers, but that was all I could summon in my memory bin that such buildings existed. Evidently, due to the magnetizing violent and drastically high loss of lives, I've become obsessed over the following years with researching and studying the nature behind the attacks. The surreality of currently being within just a few feet of the epicentre of such a historic catastrophe feels like miniature ice cubes are travelling alongside the platelets in my blood.

After a few gridlocked sessions of vehicular warfare, we pull up to the historic arena; the monstrosity of Madison Square Garden levels all who gaze upon it. In front of me, decked out in bedazzling light fixtures and towering architecture, is an iconic haven of an endless collection of concerts and sports events known to mankind. I make it inside with just enough time to spend $450 USD on an official Ranger jersey.

Row upon row in a sea of 18,000 people, the Rangers are hosting the New Jersey Devils for a mid-week matchup that brings a slew of rivalling fans across the bridge into New York. There's some history between these two teams, but nothing as crazy as what Vancouver & Boston used to be. I've been texting Ryan and Giuseppe on and off throughout the day to figure out where they're sitting. Even though Ryan told me where he was, I still had no idea where to look. I turn around and see nothing but screaming fans, strangers decked to the nines in Hockey memorabilia and winter clothing. MSG is a colossal planet, to say the least, and I'm a mere grain of sand.

Before I left my room earlier, I switched toques from Vancouver Canucks to the Chicago Blackhawks (my ex-girlfriend, Jes, had mailed this to me a few months prior. I'm continually equipping it as a mechanism to perhaps keep her memory with me even though she's been physically vacant from my life for a while).

During the game, I get in an argument with an equally as drunk idiot beside me due to wearing the Blackhawks toque and a Rangers jersey at the same time. This fortifies some type of unspeakable forbidden trail that is feared to be travelled down in the Sports World. Next, we argue about the idea of having your home team intentionally lose as many games as they can to increase their chances of securing the "Draft Lottery" the following year. This whole concept of hoping and wishing your NHL team *tanks* is entirely & utterly ridiculous. After one too many $12 piss-warm beers from the concession stand, I turn to him and say, "These athletes sacrifice their whole lives to play & pursue WINNING in the sport of their dreams so you can hope they LOSE on a consistent basis to blindly believe that obtaining some 18-year-old chump will help them win all the games of next season? The purity of the sport is 100% lessened when you have these Keyboard Generals firing off, like some deadbeat casino-dwelling hack pulling on a Slot machine, believing that this time around, 'IT'LL BE THE ONE.'" I continue, "I highly doubt when these Star performers were growing up, marching to the arena with their gear on at eight years old, that their aim was to make it to the NHL to purposely lose games to usher in some lottery STATISTIC. Wanting your home team to lose the game is moronic beyond belief. Fuck off with all this stupid nonsense, and APPRECIATE THE GAME."

In the monkey-brained hockey fan world, it is a thought-processing paradox to be representing two teams at once. I'm internally prodded, once again, reminding me that the dumbest, most intellectually void, empty-skulled idiots of our planet are those who partake in heavy alcohol use and allow themselves to become overtaken by their ego and aloofness while projecting their immovable positions on their favourite Sports teams. You just can't get any more fucking foolish.

After the game, I meet up with Ryan and Giuseppe on a different floor of Madison Square Garden. We enjoy more beers and share laughs about the differences between America and Canada. I feel fortunate to have connected with two people who share my interests in hockey and music while exploring a new city.

Learning that the two of them are staying at the same Hostel, we hitch a Cab back through Manhattan, being blinded by legions of Christmas lights plastered all over the city, racking up New York's electricity bill just another few hundred million dollars.

We make it back; they retire to their rooms.

Entirely set ablaze with mania due to the night's achievements, I take my shirt off and run down the road in the snow, looking for an Italian pizza parlour that's still open. It's -10 degrees out and has to be nearing 1 am. A small *Open* sign down the road that looks like cotton candy melted together appears to be a shop that serves fresh dough out of the oven. It draws me towards it.

"What the fuck," the Italian store owner yells in the most stereotypical mafia-sounding mush of words, "You out of your mind, kid? Where da fuck is your shirt?"

"I'm from Canada," I cockily respond, "I'm just here to try some of your best New York-style pizza."

We both howl with laughter like psychopathic wolves past their bedtime.

I carry an extra-large pizza box back to my room and find myself using it as a blanket on my bed. The dough and alcohol mixture makes me comatose and powerbombs me into a barrage of nonsensical dreams.

I'm not violently ill the next morning, possibly from finding the perfect pocket of greasy pizza distribution to help soak up the alcohol contents. Still, the quality of the air feels grotesquely stagnant at this hostel. A little fed up with the deteriorating wallpaper and less private setting, I whip out my phone and book another few days down the road at a more elegant and polished, higher-life-style hotel/complex. The upgrade was far beyond earned after putting up with shared accommodations for the last few nights (not that I really cared due to my binge drinking levels).

While waiting for the proper check-in time, I camp out in a bar and make plans to meet one of my online friends I've connected with on Instagram for years. In another hefty salute to the app Instagram for connecting me to beautiful women, my friend Alexis, who lives in New Jersey, is as eager as I am to get to finally experience each other face to face. Music is the inaugurating catalyst of almost all of my friendships. For the last two years, we've been juggling song ideas together, trying to send files back and forth like a game of hackysack. In reality, all of the other bands I've allocated time to, whatever is not dedicated to partying, swallows up any efforts of extra work on the side. She and I share the same infatuation for the band Deftones to an unrelenting degree. With our tastes being accurately compatible, while still sitting at this bar top, I go through her photos and am reminded of her magnitude of attractiveness. With a Cleopatra-like constructed glow, her dark features resemble a quasi-combination of Middle Eastern meets Italian in a flawless faceoff of bedazzling sexuality. There's no doubt my nerves are teetering off a diving board that's about to split down the middle. I know exactly what will help repair the torn fibres.

I order another drink. I phone my friend, Matthew, who's back home in Alberta, to help keep me grounded, to let loose our random conversations that touch on every subject possible, furthering our beliefs that being able to express these deep thoughts & revelations back and forth is its own form of psychotherapy/psychiatry. We will benefit from this for years to come.

After a brief stumble through the blur of city lights, I'm allowed to enter my new residence once and for all. The mini-fridge is full of various liquors and energy drinks, which I use like agility potions from an RPG game to stabilize me before Alexis makes her appearance. The potions of stabilization work, and before I know it, I'm heading back downstairs to meet Alexis on the dark streets of Brooklyn. When I see her through the hotel window, I nearly trip and do a face slide across the lobby floors. Her beauty leaves me speechless. I silently thank the liquor gods for helping me stay composed.

Our time together mirrors every phone call we've shared in the past. Over spicy-filled Ramen noodle dishes, we enjoy limitless laughter, musical debates, and all that we failed to tackle in our online chatrooms. The physical chatroom is producing a lot more sparks than I expected (after all, this was in the making for two years). After dinner, we commit to a small amount of bar hopping. I strive not to *power drink* in front of her, but I can't promise I'll keep that commitment to myself (and I don't).

As we stroll back from the bar, Alexis intertwines her fingers with mine and rests her head on my shoulder, seeking warmth from the hacking winter breeze. We move closely together through the light snowfall. All this feels like it should be working, yet I feel a mix of detached emotions, confusion, and a sense of anti-servitude to the laws of attraction. As beautiful and tempting as she is, something is missing from my radar of reality. My inner

Romeo has been bludgeoned to death by sharp memories in the shape of high heels.

We get to the front door of my hotel and part ways.

I could have invited her up to my room and made the best of coming this far across the continent. I don't want to lead her on, creating a further mess between two individuals from two different countries. I've already tried to do this with Jes in 2014. The shine of the jewels of an international relationship (or just a relationship in general) has lost its meaning of importance, its currency plummeting, remaining viciously low in my chart of values. This old thrill fails to appeal to me anymore. I have no clue what is going on with my lack of connection, affection and reflection towards getting involved with another woman. I pass out the second I get back to my room, faceplanting into the bed that's prepared like a perfectly carved cloud made of wool that was torn out of the heavens and laid out before me.

Despite having a cozy king-sized bed to rest on, the bathroom floor is the sheet of ice I wake up on the next morning. Again, I don't know because it's closer to the toilet to expel the poison from my insides, but I find myself in there over and over. I've gone hard enough on the booze for days to bring myself back to the shakes, the sickness, the resuscitated compost of disgust. The mind and body never forget. I'm left to wade through the blurry gator swamps of withdrawal for a brief moment until I eye up a small bottle of Vodka on top of the mini-fridge across the room. Pouring myself a drink mixed with 7-up at 7 AM, I turn on the News. The headlines are bold and beat red. I nearly drop my drink, both in shock and disbelief. Reports have emerged of a terrorist attack that just occurred in Manhattan. What the fuck is going on? Maybe this drink isn't strong enough.

Someone travelling near one of the train stations has just blown themselves up with a pipebomb. I intended to travel this morning to the locations shown on the hectic report. The Terrorist attack was attempted during morning rush hour to try and incapacitate as many people as possible. While he was not successful at killing anyone (or himself), multiple people were within the blast zone and had their mornings rocked to smithereens. I make one bizarre, admirable pledge to booze and convince myself that if I had not been so hungover, I could have very well been in the vicinity of that explosion. Who knows.

I raise a glass of vodka to the roof and drink it at lightning speed.

While I had planned to explore more of the city and make the most out of these experiences, this is a symbol I'll ingest to start to figure out how to get home as quickly as possible. A city once murdered with such a terrorist attack back in 2001 does not forget the abhorrent nature of such an act and will be returning fire immediately. I look down from my window perch towards the concrete jungle and notice a heavier Police presence, cop squadron cars travelling by the dozens. I'm unaware if there will be further terrorist attacks at random now that one has been unleashed. I imagine getting hacked to death via a machete or severed by an explosive device out on the streets of Brooklyn. The fear is unimaginable. Either way, it's time to get the flying fuck out of dodge and soar back to Canada. I clench my phone in a panic thinking this may land all flights or keep planes from leaving the airport. I'm pleased to realize I can still book a flight out of JFK Airport to head back to Vancouver later tonight. My heart struggles to find a calm pulse and races, dreading the escapades of getting out of here.

Committing to the return to JFK Airport, I slip into a small store and purchase a 236ml bottle of Whisky (it passed me by that such bottle sizes exist), something small enough that I feel will help put some strength back into my legs. I'm already swatting away the shakes, feeling extremely on edge as the downtown city of Brooklyn comes alive. Wheeling my belongings behind me, I hide down an alleyway off a main road to avoid getting a ticket for open alcohol use. I take a brief smell of the open lid. On cue, I projectile vomit against the alleyway walls.

You could not get more of a New York City stereotypical vision from the view down this alleyway. Dripping black ladders hanging from fixtures above. Decaying brown brick walls suffocated with wild graffiti. Steam rises out from the array of piping dispersed throughout the gutters as it does off the remnants of my stomach paste from yesterday. Dripping down the layered brick wall are the contents of whatever remained in my belly.

I gulp down the whisky and leverage my body against the cold alley wall.

I'm waiting for the alcohol to help obliterate my anxiety from existing, but it only manages to throw a weak front kick into its abdomen. The panic dissipates, but getting to the airport fries up some anxiety and singes me with its pin-pricking texture. I try and retrace my steps the way I originally came a week ago. A few skytrain rides and I'm back at the airport. Due to the terrorist attack this morning, I see armed Guards in excess patrolling the ins and outs of each terminal. As I stroll by a few of them, they arrogantly eye me up and down. In all honesty, my appearance resembles a bit of a scruff stereotypical terrorist. My dark facial features, thick and dark beard, toque pulled down, and plaid traveller clothing. *Do your worst, gentlemen.*

My flight is delayed for a few hours, perhaps due to the Terrorist attack and increased security measures around town. Even with the previously consumed whisky, invisible rats gnaw at the edges of my fingertips. I can feel the withdrawal ease its way back into my life like the odour of a missing body you've been trying to hide in the basement for weeks as detectives rummage about in your living room. I contemplate getting blackout drunk to make the plane ride tolerable, but returning to Vancouver in such a state will most likely put me behind bars. I remember the two tablets of Ativan I had in my bag. I take one and follow up with another an hour later. The support they offer helps me endure the flight and keeps my travels on track. The thickening escape rope from life puts itself in my hand and effortlessly carries me to safety on a supportive barrier.

The calming effects of Ativan make the plane engine sound like a tiger's purr. The minute I sit down in my window seat, departing towards Vancouver, I peacefully drift to sleep, knowing I will return to this city for another round of atomic escapades in the unforgiving future.

CHAPTER 10

Splinters & Cedar

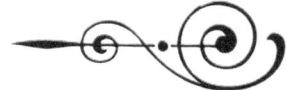

A scorcher of an August day. I awake on the sidelines of a river flowing through a mountain, far, far from home. Animals singing & empty cans clanging on sedimentary rocks like wind chimes before a brief storm. They're so out of sync with each other, kind of like musicians talking a big game before you jam with them. Black cans float on a small calm of water just below my feet. I haven't the slightest clue where I am in the world. Did I drive to Montana? Arizona? How was I able to hide my level of intoxication from the Border Guards? I've made thoughtless & exuberant long road trips before (while completely wasted) and woken up in/on different parts of the Continent. This was an easy task for me, but I was well aware of my current level of carefree degeneration. There was no way this was possible. For the last two months, I've been trying to balance my deteriorating body on a tightrope made of my own intestines. I expended all positive aspects of my life in my attempts to manage my alcohol consumption again; the most precise offering to the bottle was the loss of my girlfriend of over a year and a half. While we weren't married or had a common-law relationship spanning eight or nine years, the emotional toll of our 600 or so days together was just as achingly devasting to have ended as that of a longer-lasting union. The magnitude of this loss rivals as if she physically had died, and I can no longer see her.

The Sun is licking me like a Godzilla-sized housecat. It feels kind of cute, but I just want to backhand it away like when a real Feline is doing so. Its sandpaper tongue feels like it's removing layers of skin with each second gone by, stripping sections of my epidermis with ease. I wish there were answers to the remaining questions of catastrophe found in these UV Rays or a few ominous hints from Mother Nature to provide insight.

The weekend before this was caked with a little too much Beer & Whisky, so I switched to 7% Coolers. This matters no difference to the apocalypse. It was almost worse this way. Consuming hard alcohol would often derail me sooner and allow me to remain in one place. Gradually keeping the perfect drunk level with the use of strong Coolers enabled my manic states of unpredictability to hijack a 747, just skimming an Ocean full of undetonated mines and bloodthirsty, ravenous creatures. Incredibly belligerent with no end in sight until I drop, booze demolishes the internal GPS device, making me willingly lost at Sea with an Anchor welded to the back of my neck.

Arising to my knees, both of my hands are plunged into the sandy collection of river residue I was previously sleeping on. Across the river are rows of Lodgepole Pine Trees huddling together like the best-smelling drug users from East Hastings. To my left is a box of coolers that appears to have been torn open by a hound of hell. That hound was Me. I do a brief check of my phone, wallet, and keys. All in check. I still have no clue how I haven't lost these every time I travel down the arid corridor of intoxication.

I figured that brief power nap brought me closer to the difficulties of sobriety as my Blood Alcohol Content levels started to descend back to zero (which is a complete crapshoot of my philosophy - I am still clearly & very drunk). I reach over and crack open a drink. The sound of excellence. Where air pressure ejaculates into its surrounding vicinity and tickles the auditory canals of every Alcoholic in its presence. Though still tipsy and without care, a goofy and sick smile still finds a way to my face. There is so much going wrong, much progress in decline - I still find no reason to start caring. I begin to remember I may have driven to wherever I'm at. I need to find my car. Did I drive off a cliff and leave the vehicle to burn? I feel relatively unscathed. The hunt begins.

Getting a grand scope of the view, I appeared to have walked down a cliff face that was more dirt than rock. I saw my previous footprints and areas where I looked like I had fallen over and rolled. If there were security cameras in these woods, I'd like to rewind and watch myself do this. That thought returns to me far too often.

The climb is relatively simple. I retrace and follow the areas that I previously bailed down, like a drunk black bear manoeuvring his way through the woods. It takes me about five minutes to get to the top of the cliff. The most important thing of the short climb was to not drop a single drink in the remaining box of liquor bullets I still clutched against my chest.

Emerging through the clearing of bushes & some barren branches, the wide open highways of the Coquihala show me their vast directional highs and lows. A magnificently expansive stretch of roads connecting the Lower Mainland of British Columbia to the Interior of the Province. I'm somewhere in between the city of Hope and Merritt—hundreds of kilometres of blinding green forestry and uninhabited stillness. The stillness breaks - The hum of engine sizes ranging from 1.6L to 14.9L are making their trips upwards and downwards around me. My inner compass is misfiring like being sent onto a merry-go-round after arising from Ten rounds of boxing a Rhinoceros. The heat from the yellow globe in the sky has me squinting like waking from a months-long Hibernation.

I notice my car parked along the side of the highway near an off-ramp resting area. I remember none of this. It's parked sideways. Completely engulfed in the misery of anti-sobriety, I stumble to my car, unlock the door, and fall into the driver's seat.

I purchased this Pontiac G6 three months earlier due to drunkenly leaving my previous vehicle at my Parent's house. I was too mangled and far too riddled with anxious debilitation to manage to try and drive my other car back from Abbotsford to Vernon (roughly a four-hour, 400km drive), so I travelled via E-Bus back to the Okanagan. While this current whip was nothing special to write home about, it was a much more powerful upgrade than my previous tiny Hyundai Accent, which I had to purchase on a budget due to the 2021 Sumas Prairie Floods destroying another vehicle of mine (also almost killing my Dog and I... perhaps another story for another book). With this Pontiac, a V6 engine of 225hp and a body design that was much lower to the road, destinations were all too easy to make it to with time to spare.

Ignition turned on. Tunes full blast. I depart from this pointless stop in my travels, trying to make it back to Kamloops (another two hours North). I barely remember leaving the wide parkade. The road begins to climb up to the clouds. Functionality fades.

I regain my memory as I drive past Merritt, a town about an hour north of where I previously was. I'm starting to get a gist of where I'm at, though I'm drifting in and out of a drunken stupor. How is it possible that I'm driving normally (or so I believe) between the lines of the highway at such a high speed? The permanency of Death follows from behind me every millisecond while being on the road in such a state. Music floods my car like a sexual partner you're fed up with but can't seem to remove from your life. I switch between songs from unhinged Death Metal to the most melancholic of despair-ridden emotional tunes. I forget where I'm heading. A blank slate. Almost like a state of meditation but poisoned with pellets of fear. Where am I going? Why are my hands on the steering wheel, and I'm travelling at 140kmh? Nonsensical. I lose focus, drifting into a blackout.

CHAPTER 11

Onyx Waves

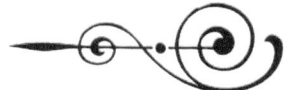

Two and half months have flown by relatively peacefully. Aside from the nightmare of travelling blackout drunk all around Abbotsford to Kamloops in the Summer, overall clarity has evened itself out. Being able to detox myself from my previous onslaught of alcohol by titrating my consumption with beers as a remedy (this has been performed and is still being done in some countries under the supervision of a physician), I've been able to place my shoes on the proper feet and reel my life into the arms of regularity. When I felt ready to give it up, I began to apply some feverish formula for decreasing my alcoholic intake per day. Starting with 15 beers on Monday, 13 on Tuesday, 12 on Wednesday, 10 on Thursday, and so on and so forth. Eventually (still with severe discomfort and irritating insomnia), one can manage to come off of Alcohol by investing resources into this procedure. Modern medical professionals do not recommend this process of a self-detox, but whatever dignity I had left was not going to be found in a hospital setting, deteriorating with other forms of death all around me.

It takes just over a week, but success soon will be found. I've also found solace in full-time work again, a structured balance of all my creative outlets, honouring my time spent in the gym, musical creation, and socializing with possible new girlfriends (though that remains to be my introduction to a downfall when letting this into my life too early). However, I've grown a new layer of ignorance around my skin that has gotten bored of this pointless routine.

I get far too cocky one week and ask my co-worker, Cheyenne, out for friendly drinks. She has no clue of the extent of how powerful my addiction to Alcohol is, and I'm not ready to relay that information to her in fine detail. 10% of me feels like I securely have my hands on the Horns of Mephistopheles and can ride this night into the next day unscathed. The other 90% is so bloody disingenuous with me, ignoring the safety flares sent down by entities waving SOS signals in my face.

I am snared back into the cycle of psychological irresponsibility.

Day 13 or 14 of being submerged in a trench of all that is 5%, 14%, and 40% diabolical fluid. I'm rattled awake at 4:30 am, arising from infinite nothingness. Very rarely do any dreams occur in intoxicated sleep. The nightmares will come. This I'm very aware of. Sadly, the current plague is that the morning withdrawals have now become devastatingly challenging to manage. This morning, I have no booze left. I pounded it all back last night. The dreaded waiting until 9 am (when liquor stores open) legitimately feels like watching yourself have open heart surgery with inexperienced surgeons while you're awake. Here and now, the mind is transfixed on anything that has to do with ethanol. It has become the saviour and grace that is also an online snuff video of yourself captured by Terrorists, decapitating you on live feed for the world to see.

A fire hydrant of Sulfuric Acid erupts in my brain. Fear. Seismic chart registering shaking. I begin to lose touch with my surroundings. At any moment, my heart feels as if it'll squirm its way through my ribcage and eject out of my chest. Every thought feels like a multitude of blisters rapidly multiplying and exploding. Maybe I'm finally going to have a seizure.

Amongst this crisscross feeling like running into traffic with my entire body ablaze, I remembered my Roommate having a Mickey of Honey flavoured Jack Daniels sitting in the Kitchen. Though time feels like it does not even exist, it's ticking and ticking fast. I bolt for my bedroom door amidst the clink & clang of vodka and wine bottles colliding with each other on the floor.

Still holding a flame of decency for others, I try not to make noise on my way to the Kitchen (near impossible in this state), as my Roommate and Landlords are still sleeping upstairs. It's about 5 am, and here I am, looking to drink everything in sight as if it's New Year's Eve and the clock is about to roll over.

Glistening in the dim Kitchen lights like morning frost being punctured by the Sunrise, I scope out the bottle of Jack Daniels.

My god. It's one of the most beautiful things I've ever seen. Even just the sight of dormant Alcohol within reach provides me with lush comfort. The sight of it is no comparison to its taste in desperate times like these.

My hand struggles to vigorously spin the cap off the bottle.

Like a novelty spinning Top or those ridiculous BeyBlades toys from the early 2000s, It comes flying off. There's that aroma; certifiably famous for its strong chemical structure, Jack Daniels holds one of the most recognizable and punctual scents in the Liquor business.

Slam.

In a pendulum-style motion, I drink from the bottle in two quick swigs. Similar to dropping a bowling ball onto a trampoline, the two shots wiggle their way down my esophagus, pausing for a moment and then projecting back up. Luckily, I'm near the kitchen sink, and the vomit finds itself split across the sink like da Vinci found himself painting a Money Shot.

I have no clue about the contents inside of the puke. Black tar pudding sprinkled with red chunks of hemorrhaging soil. There's no time to try and analyze if I'm spewing blood from my insides. I'm gasping for air and clutching the sink to not collapse to the floor in convulsions. The first drink after a night of heavy intoxication almost always backfires. In order to keep it down, there's a sequence of allowing yourself to reject it actively and following it up in quick succession with another. I try this out. Right after puking, I take another longer swig and gaze at the roof. Blurred vision from swollen eyes full of salt. It takes a mere 90 seconds for the contents of Alcohol to pass through the Blood

Brain Barrier and circulate through your body. These are some of the longest seconds known to Man. The overwhelming flood of toxic substances at an alarming rate while battling dehydration, malnutrition and flawed sleeping patterns would seem like it is the last thing one would want to partake in, but that couldn't be further from the truth. This is the nurturing Mother stabilizing me after a night of hysteria and bloodshed. With each passing moment, I start to feel a slight tickle/massage-like sensation behind my ears. A warming glow of such magnitude provided me with razor-sharp scissors right before I was about to be hung from the gallows.

Chemically, it works its magnificent magic. Breathing becomes steady. Muscles loosen. My eyelids slightly droop a little lower. No longer do I feel as if Hornets are coating my throat and a Grizzly bear is eyeing me up to stretch my intestines around a redwood tree. Evenly paced waves lap around me after my whole life's water vessel took a mile-long iceberg to its hull. The calm is here.

There was no time to mix a drink of better-tasting proportions due to the face-ripping dreadful cataclysm of withdrawing. Now that that is over, I mix myself a strong glass with some leftover Diet Pepsi from the fridge. I giggle to myself, trying to picture someone ordering this kind of drink at the bar. With a smile on their face, "Yeah, I'll get three shots of JD and a slight spritz of flat Pepsi together, please. No ice. Thanks."

Here is a sign of returning to the self. The Alcohol returns to its governing chair and has a seat holding the heavy weapons. My goofy humour returns to its natural state. My anxiety, which previously had me naked and about to be gutted & dropped into a sea of ravenous sharks, takes off. It's walking away, and I'm giving it two middle fingers as it looks back at me.

Fuck off and never return, please.

That's wishful thinking. I know it'll be back in roughly eight to twelve hours if I don't keep the alcohol titrated like a medicinal bag of wonders injected into my bloodstream. I had just gone from feeling like my skeleton was sharpening its bones, trying to dash away from my skin, tissue, and flesh, to now feeling like there are a group of paradisal Angels smothering me with their affinity.

I've stopped responding to those reaching out to me from my job. Usually, the first few days are phone calls, which leads to emails/texts, which leads to just turning my phone off or ignoring the messages altogether. I feel nothing from sympathizers. Why is help ignored as the descent to a non-returnable, oneway trip to Hell begins to take place? I've never been actively suicidal. If I was being torched to death in a vehicular accident, my skin bubbling around me, and an arm reached in to pull me out, I would accept the help. If I were carrying a shotgun, noticing a murderous figure following me home in the pitch dark, wielding a machete and stating it was going to make mincemeat of my body, I would light it up and not stop until I was guaranteed of its demise. I've built such a strong backbone around my safety & the safety of others being such a priority - so why is it that I voluntarily allow Alcohol to kill me and those around me?

Holding my hand out in front of me in a regular fashion like hundreds of nights before, I notice the shaking has subsided, and a strange, beautiful, but ominous feeling rains over me. It's like having the impossible option of being half exposed in an Antarctic outpost and the other half standing in an Australian outback pitstop. The cold. The warmth. The heat. It's almost indescribable. My body is trying to make sense of its environment. It slides the puzzle pieces gone awry into some kind of presentable fashion.

The entire day is ahead of me. I'm standing in my boxers in a dimly lit Kitchen at 5:30 am with a drink in my grasp. I've started this morning out with close to four or five shots of Whisky. Typically, this would piledrive the average being on their ass. As they'd go to tie their shoes outside, they'd most likely stumble back up with an imprint of concrete on their forehead. Not me. As standard as the generic cup of coffee, Alcohol becomes my go-to early morning Breakfast to project me into oblivion. I often cycle between wine or hard liquor when the going gets rough. Trying to make sense of life when all you have are 5% measly cans of liquid bread is far too colourful and violent. Shotgunning is almost out of the question as your hands fumble and all of the remnants spray around you like the most pressurized jugular vein being exposed to outer elements. The upheavals are five times as bad, and it takes much longer to feel stationed upright on this Earth. What terrifies me the most is succumbing to a Grand Mal Seizure while trying to do everything in my power to fight it off. Not all Alcoholics will have this happen to them, but it's been medically documented enough to instill fear into all of the shaky hands that are trapped in this soul-stripping state of disharmony.

I left a $20 bill where the bottle of Jack Daniels was resting. I never enjoy leeching off people. I say a small thanks of gratitude to my Roommate. His keeping of this bottle for so long may have just saved my life. Now, with more pace in my steps, I walk back into my bedroom and sit at the edge of my bed. I feel like I've been transferred into the body of the world's most outstanding athlete. Just an hour ago, I was having difficulty breathing & moving four feet in front of me. This is an unbelievable transformation I'll undergo year after year, drink after drink.

Two or three years ago, I had unsuccessfully tried to halt my chaotic drinking habits with medical interventions. I still keep the remnants of pharmaceuticals (Benzodiazepines) with me. As noted before, these medications are used to ease withdrawal and prevent further complications. A few pills of Valium here and there. Gabapentin to reduce the possibility of seizures. A small amount of Ativan powder collected in a urine-coloured pill bottle. Never have I had an issue with any sort of Pills or harder drugs. To this day, it surprises me that I never struggled with anything else. Just as a safety blanket, I keep these pills in one of the travel bags I've brought around with me from city to city. During this current bender, for some bizarre reason, I begin to experiment with furthering the quest for the ultimate GABA receptor overcharged experience. Before bed, even though I had plentiful Alcohol in my body, faced with Alcoholic delusions and thinking I could pull myself out of this hell, I would crush a small pill of Gabapentin and snort it viciously through one nostril. I knew the contents were minor enough, and it would be enough to calm me down for the night. However, once again, mixing both Benzodiazepines and Alcohol (especially at my rate of consumption) is a bullet train to the graveyard. It's a 5-star concoction to be blitzed beyond recognition. Nobody else is riding this out-of-control train except me.

Mobile Delivery services have now become my drug dealers. The moment both hands of the clock meet at 9 am, I'm actively on my phone choosing what alcohol to have delivered to my front door. What an absolute lottery for the hardcore drinker.

As my body reaches a regular norm of having the whisky contents swim through me, my hunger returns after not eating for a day or two. Again, more unhealthy choices of greasy hamburgers, wings, and other pub food are increasingly stimulated in my mind as dozens of restaurant options flash before my swollen eyes on smartphone apps.

Just a few weeks ago, I was maintaining a highly rigorous diet of clean, high-protein foods, a variety of balanced carbohydrates, and my regular plethora of adequate amino acids.

Having been going to the gym four to five days a week, the muscle tone I was able to achieve over time is slowly chipped away by these cargo loads of unhealthy preferences.

Losing Valerie in the Summer crushes my insides with brick after brick of cauterizing railroad spikes.

Most days begin to blend together, and I'm starting to lose track of when it's daytime or nighttime. There is a small window in my bedroom that shines minimal sunlight or moonlight due to the way it's facing. The only thing holding me in the realm of reality is ensuring my iPhone is plugged in to stay in contact with the outside world. Often, I wake up from blacking out to find it is dead. The deterioration of the core of my soul begins.

Whenever I open my banking app, dread nearly disembowels me. My money is running out, as are the pounds off my body. I have never really struggled with weight issues my entire life, but things get out of hand rapidly as I go from 200 pounds down to 185 in a matter of two to three weeks. Every three to four months of crippling effort I've previously spent at the gym is wiped away in a matter of a dozen or so days.

I become far too comfortable with watching Pornography in an excessive amount on my iPhone. All of this alcohol stimulates a section of my brain that becomes over-occupied with it. Though it is nowhere near the extent as far in the group I was paired with in rehab back in 2018, the alcohol does alter a section of my brain to become fixated on it. I'll start to *sext* Women who I've known for years through a series of strange text messages. Some shut me down immediately, some are the opposite, saying, "I've been waiting for this for so long." Who knew, even in such retched states of disparity, that sexual interest would still be flourishing? I've committed myself to a self-made psychiatric hospital void of functionality and any outcomes of hope.

I still have enough strength to make it to the bathroom in time. In my current state of mind, I've never woken up with urine-soaked sheets (yet). That makes me slightly proud in a highly pathetic sort of way.

My Social Media posts are scarce, but when they do emerge, they are often deadly cryptic and create a vital concern for my friends and family. I feel this is a proper time for me to post explicit and shocking lyrics from some of my poems written over time—a whole-hearted way to invoke worry in those around me. A passionately violent post was made one night on my Facebook feed, leading to the morning of me rushing to delete it due to embarrassment and fear one of my friends would phone the Police to hunt me down. What does an Artist do once they've captured a moment of self-reflection encased in a jumble of words, thoughts, and writings? They project it to their surroundings, the beam on their lighthouse, to be seen & heard from the world outside.

Empty brown paper bags litter the floor below my bed, looking like I've tried to redo the carpeting to give it more of a homeless look. I've depleted the last of my resources on a few bottles of wine to have delivered to the house. As my phone notifies me that the delivery has arrived, I head upstairs to grab it. My landlord, Steve, is upstairs for a stint at home, away from work for a few days. As I go to retrieve it, I'm greeted by him in the hallway. He's holding the bags full of wine. I can't tell if he realizes what is going on, but there is an annoyed/concerned look in his facial expression that has me on edge. I thanked him and brought the contents back to my room. Hours go by of shooting back liquid grapes like an army from the Dark Ages ready to embark on their final pillaging and plundering spree.

Somewhere around 8 pm, even though battered with the depressant effects of booze, there is a subsiding of negative emotions that transforms into a sliver of courage (after all, I'm well aware of the term *liquid courage* flaunting its definition). After numerous requests and acts of kindness from friends and family reaching out to me, I commit to critical help. I can no longer engage in these escapades, as one night, I might not wake up at all.

I had just sold my car a few weeks prior to this (using that $3,000 I made from it to feverishly keep me in this dooming drinking spell), so the option of driving to a clinic was out of the question. I have no choice but to call an ambulance. I await their presence as I sit on the edge of my bed, trying to keep my wits about me.

Hearing a few words being exchanged from upstairs, I stumble towards the noise. My landlord, who appears visibly upset, is speaking with the ambulance driver. I walk up to the both of them.

"What the hell, man?" questions Steve, "You could have just told me you needed a ride."

"It's all good, man," I arrogantly assure him, "I'll be back. I just have to take care of this."

He's standing beside his Wife, who is equally as confused. They don't know what to think. There's no guarantee that they can probably smell the alcohol protruding from my pores, but it's a given they're aware of what's been transpiring over the last few weeks.

I've tried limiting my alcohol intake throughout the day and night, which ironically makes me more and more sick as it filters through my liver and out of my bloodstream.

What is killing me makes me more ill as I try to come out of its murderous clutches. Go figure.

In the back of the ambulance, I vomit into a plastic puke bag. Wisps of gloomy city lights flash by the windows. Nauseating belches rumble through my stomach and out of my mouth. These are some of the most disgusting and degrading moments of my life.

All of the successes I achieved years ago visit me for brief moments in my memory bank and then execute themselves with a polished revolver for the world to see. Past the point of no return, I do my best to remain focused on the task at hand - to engage as diligently as possible to quit alcohol for good.

I get to the Hospital ER and thank the driver for bringing me here.

I feel the unbearable weight against my arms. My eyes are bloodshot red from lack of sleep and limp as if miniature weights are balanced on my lashes. I look like complete and total miserable shit. I'm left to wait, sitting in a chair against the entrance to the Emergency Room. Minutes pass. 30 minutes. 45 minutes. This feels like a complete waste of time. I think back to having done this before. While there is still alcohol in my system, many Hospitals don't take it as seriously due to my BAC (Blood Alcohol Content) not being at 0.00%. The literature on Alcohol Withdrawal has strongly shown even just a slight decrease in ethanol (in heavy drinkers) in the blood can cause a patient to start to undergo withdrawal (for example, someone who regularly maintains a BAC of around 0.31 to 0.41 will begin to feel a variety of uncomfortable symptoms as the ethanol is processed through the Liver receding to 0.12 to 0.15, eventually leading to 0.00 which throws all of it into a razor-wind of horrors).

Feelings of unease poke around in my ribcage.

I momentarily think about having to stay in this hospital for a few days to come off of this and bail on my original plan.

I can do this myself by titrating down and tapering slowly off the drink. After all, I've just done this a few months back. I've made this a concrete plan and have been able to walk away from it a new man (though successfully doing it cleanly and without a mental illness-inducing amount of pain is impossible). I know the hell that awaits.

I slump over to the front desk, telling the woman behind the glass that I can't do this tonight. Ripping off my wristband given to me earlier, I walk out of the facility. Feeling like a *Wish version* of Einstein with this new plan of mine, I limp towards the liquor store a few blocks from the hospital. This impending strike of withdrawal shakes is starting to trip up my footsteps. Quick and efficient, I enter the store and find my typical 12-pack of strong Neutral Coolers, my go-to evil Brothers in battle. I feel around for my wallet and am left standing there like a complete idiot. I must have left it at home on my dresser.

Slightly feeling a murderous rush of anxiety, I whip up a plan to try and pay with my phone. Sprawling both my arms into the air in a plea for my life, I asked the attendant behind the counter if I could send him $45 via E-transfer on our phones so he could pay for this package of drinks. Expecting to get kicked out of the store, he agrees to accept the transfer.

Thinking about the booze sends more shivers through my skin. Right as I transferred the money to him, my phone died.

I grab the Alcohol and leave.

Exiting the store and bringing myself back to the drink, I laugh for a minute, realizing there will be no archaic payphones that I can slip a few quarters into to make a call with.

I stop at a pizza shop down the road for a brief moment and ask the chap behind the counter to call a Taxi. Pondering whether or not I'll be able to pull off another stint of detoxing by myself, I relax in an empty stall at the entrance of the store. The employees of the store should have been yelling at me not to consume alcohol in public, but no one mouthed a word. I fail to care, either.

During the cab ride back to the Northwest side of town, I inform the driver that I'll need to dash inside to retrieve my wallet once we arrive.

We pull into my driveway.

"I'm sorry about all this," I plead to him, "I'll be right back with the money."

I'm feeling relatively returned to normal. The wonders of drunken, nonchalant wanderings overtake me.

As I head downstairs to search for my wallet, I notice my guitar against the wall, in its case, at the front door. My Landlord, Steve, and my roommate, Joel, are hauling things out of my room in garbage bags at a panicked rate.

"What the hell is going on here?" I loudly ask.

"There's no way you can stay here, man," Steve yells as he marches by me with bags of my belongings, "We never agreed to have an addict move into this house."

The fact that these two have entered my bedroom without permission casts an unspeakable amount of wrath around my nerve endings. Neither of these Men has the legal right to enter my room without written or verbal consent. Steve's choice of words are harsh. He is being relatively rude and upfront. I make a few pleas for understanding, but none of them are being accepted.

Joel retreats to his room and closes the door. I'm left in the living room to face Steve.

"Look," I assure him, "I have an alcohol problem that I'm working to exterminate for good. I just need a bit of time to figure this out."

"I don't care how much time you need," Steve replies, "you're going to have to find somewhere else to do it."

My two-month stay at this house has been nothing but calm, collected, quiet and respected.

He and I have had many amicable conversations, and I was starting to feel I could consider him a friend.

I feel my insides being gouged at from my backside—a complete stab in the back.

"How the fuck can you just walk into my room without telling me and haul my personal belongings to the outside elements? Do you know how much that guitar costs to me?" I yell at Steve with more gunpowder in my voice than before.

Steve is unwillingly stubborn and makes a multitude of more rude comments, calling me an addict and someone with problems that no one in his household needs to be around.

He has a solid point on his latter defence, but the name-calling and epithets are uncalled for and have given me fuel for a vicious fight. He goes as far as to call me a *junkie*, something I take heavy offence to. Though I have been trapped in a deep rut of alcoholism for the last few weeks, the uprooting call to arms brings the organ-spilling Lion from within me out of its Den and a package of fresh blood beneath its nostrils.

Being taller, heavier, and reminiscing of my training at an MMA gym I used to live at the previous year, I could kick the living fucking tar out of this guy.

It rapidly crosses my mind as I figure out where to store this prominent rage.

We argue back and forth for a good 30 minutes.

Is it worth it for me to just strangle him and throw his lifeless corpse out in the snow outside?

I'm aware that his Wife is upstairs. Knowing this keeps me from entirely losing self-control and creating unspeakable harm.

He calls his Brother to come home from work to help process this situation. They want me out of the house, but in all terms of legality, they have failed to adhere to the Tenancy Act/Housing Contract I signed with them upon moving in. They are required to provide me with a 24-hour notice before entering my room. They've gone ahead and barged through my Tenant rights and entered on their behalf. The fact they've carelessly decided to do so, plus putting their hands on my belongings, does not bide well with me.

I'm locked in my fighting stance, and if someone wants to lay a hand on me, their fucking jugular will be ripped to the roof. I'm not going anywhere.

It takes his Brother another hour to get home.

I'm willfully waiting for a two-on-one brawl of fist-filled proportions.

I hold my ground and clench my fists.

Steve and I are still engaging in verbal semantics when his brother comes barrelling down the stairs, screaming at me,

"You need to leave RIGHT NOW!"

"Just fucking try to make me," I yell as I outstretch my arms, casually walking back into my old room, now void of any objects.

After having been lawfully removed from my old house with my ex-girlfriend, Valerie, this same year back in June, the feeling of becoming a voiceless servant once again is not a role I wish to take.

I'm revisiting old feelings of how worthless that made me feel. I'm electrified with more savagery.

Sober me would work through this situation and come out ahead, creating a clean exit path and with the least resistance possible (though, I would never allow myself to face such interactions, to begin with, if not drinking, but drunk me is on the brink of psychopathy, an all-out cement-headed goon taking no changes of pace and no bullshit).

Both Brothers are visibly mortified. All it takes is one ounce of physical touch, and it's time to rumble. I know my rights well enough to know they've been toyed with.

Everything I own has been placed into large construction site garbage bags that are now sitting either in the hallway upstairs or outside in the snow. I think of my custom Taylor Acoustic guitar (though, in its case) being damaged by the elements of the cold. More rage licks my insides.

I close the door and sit in fury.

I've totally forgotten about the Taxi driver outside. This blankets me with feelings of guilt. The guilt disintegrates back into the understanding of feral animalism.

Behind the closed bedroom door, I hear Steve and his brother phoning 911. I egg them on to do their worst.

Roughly 45 minutes transpire before two large police officers are at the doorstep of my room.

I went over my situation with both of them, hoping for a resolution to this absurdity.

Will the notion of goodwill return to my side in moments of peril? Errors persist and will forever remain in that signal for help.

I'm placed under arrest for criminal mischief.

I can sense in the voices from the Officers that they, too, believe I'm not entirely in the wrong, but they want to apply their best situational diffusing skills to what's happening tonight.

I maniacally laugh out loud. This makes zero sense to me as all I have been doing is exercising my right as someone who legally paid as a tenant yet has had said rights shoved up one's own ass.

Both Officers usher me out of the bedroom.

Before I leave, I request to be able to slam one more drink. Before they can even answer, I polish off a whole can of a 7% Neutral.

As I leave, I tell both of the Brothers I wish for them to be incinerated in the underworld.

Upon leaving, I wish I had taken the rest of my drinks with me. I have a feeling the Cops would not allow it.

It takes everything in me not to want to throw a right cross punch to one of their faces, specifically Steve.

I hold back.

I've processed just enough alcohol to feel stabilized for a few hours, but as I'm hauled to jail, a different sort of sickness punches me in the face: an emotional illness.

We get to the police station. I'm placed in a damp and rank concrete squared room with the door locked behind me. Piss and repugnant, continuously returning whiffs of mould scour around.

I notice a steel slab and a dark blue plastic sheet that they call a *blanket*.

Waiting for the morning to come is one of the most miserable experiences of my entire life. Not only will I have to face the appalling withdrawal, but I'm also not sure if I'm being charged with mischief and will be transferred to Prison.

To add to my discomfort, the cell beside mine is host to a belligerent and obnoxious lunatic screaming at one of the guards for hours on end. I drift in and out of consciousness with my arm over my face to try and grab any ounce of darkness due to the blinding, full-blast security lights soaking the room. I've never felt like such a sewer creature like I have now.

All I hear is the sink on the toilet dripping and the goofball down the hall spit and froth at the mouth. If he were in my cell, I most likely would have choked him unconscious, perhaps even going as far as to kill him.

Six or seven hours pass. The rapid-fire dreams and visions I've been having are insanely damaging, and I feel like there's sandpaper cleansing the insides of my head. Not being sure whether it is still dark outside or the next morning, an officer rattles on the door and wakes me from what feels like a schizophrenic slumber.

"So, Jordan," says the cop as he leans against the wall, ready to retire from his night shift, "Do you normally sleep with a machete beside your bed? This terrified your landlords."

When my landlords entered my bedroom, they bore witness to the helpless state I kept the room in. The unclean turmoil of paper bags, liquor bottles, and clothes everywhere gave them the right to invoke worry. That same night before I had left the house, I took an array of darkened photos of myself with a camping machete I purchased months prior. The way the room looked captured the essence of the disgusting moments of my personal hell. I would never in my life threaten anyone in that household with the knife that I owned. My previous Landlord had assumed I was a threat between the walls of his home. As I sober up, I understand his reasoning and feel slight guilt.

Feeling the shakes come on, I don't have time to listen to this bullshit.

"Sir," I chime in, "you're an officer of the law. Do you not sleep with a weapon beside you? I do a lot of hiking and exploring around the rivers. There's nothing wrong with having a machete with you for defence."

He doesn't answer my question. Instead, he tells me that the brothers have decided not to charge me for last night's charades. I can't even smile at that fact. I desperately need a drink to keep myself from snapping. To me, the Officer's voice resembles mumbled frequencies rather than coherent English. I've lost track of what's happening. I'm well aware telling the Cop about my withdrawal situation will invoke no sympathy, and I have to let this pan out on its own.

I've brought nothing with me for them to confiscate. I lost my phone when I was exiting the Taxi the previous night, and my wallet is still nowhere to be found. In this day and age, leaving any building to the outside world without your Phone and Wallet is similar to stargazing with a blindfold on— it just doesn't look or feel right.

The Officer wishes me luck, escorts me through the Police Station, and closes the door.

Like a stealth bomber appearing overhead, the approaching Winter climate of Kamloops multiplies the anxiety.

Before leaving Jail, I noticed the clock read 8:30 am. By the time I'm able to find a liquor store, it should be just about time to open up. Those glorious neon lights screaming at me, "OPEN!"

Without currency to bring me the salvation of liquor, I'm left in a vicious battle of whether I should just enter the store and openly drink what's on the shelf. Doing this will bring me back to jail. Mentally, I'm a crumbling skyscraper trying to be held upright.

With one other option left to save me from succumbing to god knows what due to this incoming state of possible delirium, I follow whichever way I believe the hospital to be.

I pass by a beautiful woman with warm coffee in her hands, the steam of the brew rising to her flawless face. I ask which way the hospital is. She points south and quickly walks in the other direction. My zombified appearance does her well for scrambling for safety.

After a few minutes of trying not to collapse against the piercing cold concrete, I recognize the outer shell of a building ahead of me. The all too familiar blood-red letters spelling "EMERGENCY" glow above.

I vomit in the soil against one of the outside trees.

Shuttering and shivering, not from the weather but from withdrawal, I fade into the ER entrance and take a leap into reformatting what was once an energetic and valuable life.

CHAPTER 12

Cloud Splitter

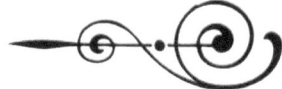

December 2022
Kamloops, B.C., Canada

A 30W floor heater bleeds its miniature thermogenic waves across my motel room as I ponder why the central heating is not working on one of the coldest snaps the city of Kamloops has seen for years. The heater looks like a conglomerate of LED Carrots glowing from a tiny sphere found in a junkyard. It's -37 degrees outside. I'm on the edge of a beaten Motel mattress, texting an addictions counsellor who I've been paired up with after completing a Seven-day stay in a Detox facility in town. Before Detox, I had been admitted to the hospital for four days. Remaining in a hospital setting was paramount to making it through another round of catastrophic states of withdrawal. My stay there was agonizing. Brief visions south of heaven are becoming more colourful and barbaric.

I'm not sure if my body and mind were being suctioned to different realms, formidable areas of Hell, but I survived.

Throughout the course of recovering from the previous weeks, I've been placed into a strong network circle of healthcare workers. Strangely enough, they've connected me with an extremely attractive female Social Worker, Madeline, who's around six years younger than I am. I had realized she was going to be female due to her name on the papers they had given me after leaving, but there was no indication in these documents of her level of attractiveness. They could have given me a stronger warning on that.

Slender and flawless. Hand-picked from a group of celestial beings and crafted into feminine form. Medium-long straight blonde hair. The sort of Southern State-looking stereotype beauty queen you'd break your neck spinning your head 180 to get a glimpse of. Recovering from the whole detox experience & being immersed into reality, once again, I'm finding it difficult to concentrate when I'm speaking with Madeline. It took me five minutes to find her pictures on Facebook. We've gone out on two or three tea dates/meetings to formulate a projection plan for myself. In the Health field, this is seen as a Social Worker meeting with an Addict. In my eyes, I'm channelling this as an experience to get to know her more. I'm looking blindly past the obvious totems of this situation and start to harvest a slight crush on her. I haven't been around or spent any significant amount of time talking to a Female one-on-one, covering deep topics of my past. She's always attentive and seems to contain some hidden healing spells for the wounds I reveal. This is the first time in years I've felt someone actually processing my information and working on it. Even in my previous failing relationship with Valerie, I often felt my words resembled rubber ping-pong balls off of her, never being truly receptive.

Madeline and I exchange a few more text messages as the mulish icicle blitz of December stirs about. It's nearly as cold inside this Motel room as it is outside. My bedroom window is a complete sheet of ice. The outside street lamps cut through the glass, looking like Lemon Quartz being smudged into the process of liquefaction.

I've been sober for 30 days, but it's looking like I'm going to beat both those numbers senseless with a snow shovel and begin the decline. Marching down the flesh-made steps to an infinite Hell takes very few decisions to start its descent.

Before I entered Detox at the end of November, I'd just left my eighth job in less than five and a half years. I could have had a long & promising (but still windy) path of success in each company. This routine becomes like dysfunctional clockwork. At first, a rainstorm of remorse finds me for a few hours, contemplating whether or not I should put down the drink and force a workday with a severe hangover (which I would do consistently from 2010 to 2017). The other part of me begins to ransack those around me with fierce resentment, maximizing the worst (from nothing), issuing myself the right to spew acidic thoughts left, right, and centre, giving me some bizarre state of manic-rising power, all guided by the contents of ethanol in a glass bottle. I chime with the latter. I'm well aware finding work has never brought me too many complications, so I roll with it. The world of Trades is constantly blooming, and bodies are needed to further its reproduction across this country of Canada. I consider myself lucky to have decided, at 18 years old, to enter the Heavy Duty Trucking Industry as a Parts Technician. It has been financially rewarding and has carried me through life without having to attend University, which would give my cortisol levels a rocket to the moon due to buckling student debt & the gruelling schedule of classroom bullshit.

I do attribute the struggle with substance abuse to my Career norms for accepting it for *what it is*.

I've never been fired from any status of work. Instead, I'll try to cloak myself from my issues, briefly discussing them with whoever the manager I'm talking to at whichever job, and bail. Admitting I have a problem was never a vital issue of mine. I'm pretty sure at 20 years old; I was able to look at my drinking patterns and come clean about how murderous it was becoming. I'm not one of those degenerates who have lived a life of incalculable losses due to Alcohol consumption, and still, to the day, they say, "I do not have a problem." What was more dangerous with my experiences was admitting to the problem and doing nothing about it—a very minimal effort of doing nothing staggeringly forceful towards change.

Without a driver's license, no stable income, and relying on minimal savings to stay afloat in this Lusifcer-created Lake of Lobotomization, I've begun to question if there's any reasoning behind remaining sober. My commitment to the gym, a positive dietary outlook/plan, and starting to lock in deeper sleep is what keeps my head glued to my body. I'm starting to read more books and can retain the pages consumed mentally. A healthy routine keeps everything looking reasonably lustrous. Still, much like many who struggle with substance, there's a specific time window of around 25 to 100 days where the possibility of relapsing remains the highest.

It takes me nearly three and a half hours to get to the gym and back when it should take no longer than 20 minutes (if I had my license). Forging around town via City Transit is a feeling like no other; loaded with shady characters, the moist and damp pungent reek of oil & piss-filled snow, body odour, unadulterated noise, filth and unhygienic strangers. Everything is always wet. It's ironic that I even complain about this when I become all of these (and more) abhorrent aromas when rotting at the bottom of the barrel. My license being stripped from me in the Summertime consumes me with feral rage.

My driver's license was cancelled on me after I admitted to a hospital nurse that I preferred to drink and drive to battle my withdrawals and road anxiety. Though they never caught me in the act of doing so, I still feel the action was uncalled for and entirely unfair (but it very well may have saved my life). Either or, loathsome resentment boils.

While I walk through saltless sidewalks & barren roads of downtown Kamloops, often almost falling with each trip into town due to the slippery & snowy atmosphere of minus-zero weather, little ambition stirs in my festering pot of peril. A Doctor who I previously was speaking with in Detox, supposedly more versed in addictions, prescribed me two medications for alcohol dependence that have been studied over the past decade. This past month, I've begun taking Baclofen and Naltrexone. Baclofen is a medication used to treat muscle spasticity, mainly for those suffering from conditions like spinal cord lesions and multiple sclerosis, so being offered it at first had me more than confused (which should have evolved into fear.. as if I needed to balance any more substances that can produce dependency, Baclofen can create a withdrawal syndrome which can also become life-threatening). Before taking it, I go over the precautions found on a white sheet of paper provided with the medication. It reads, "Withdrawal symptoms may include auditory hallucinations, visual hallucinations, tactile hallucinations, delusions, confusion, agitation, delirium, disorientation, fluctuation of consciousness, insomnia, dizziness, nausea, inattention, memory impairments, perceptual disturbances, itching, anxiety, depersonalization, hypertonia, hyperthermia, formal thought disorder, psychosis, mania, mood disturbances, restlessness, and behavioural disturbances, tachycardia, seizures, tremors, autonomic dysfunction, hyperpyrexia (fever), extreme muscle rigidity resembling neuroleptic malignant syndrome and rebound spasticity." They forgot to summarize that into a few words; "Take this, and we'll try to help put you to sleep for good." That's one hell of a fire-stoking and innard-churning warning to swallow.

Withdrawing from Alcohol takes all the previously listed symptoms and amplifies them through murderous surges of electrical activity. To pair the two together is an invitation to have your throat slit with a butcher's cleaver.

Baclofen activates GABA receptors found in the brain, slightly similar to what Alcohol produces, therefore adapting to a similar procedure of withdrawal if dependence is formed (again, taking this medication for a mere month is enough to establish said dependence). As per the antics of the pharmaceutical companies attaching pills on the ends of hooks aimed at human mouths, it has been documented as an off-label medication to combat alcohol cravings. I feel like a prodded rat looking for small scraps of food around a cage overseed by looming shadows in lab coats. Naltrexone, often used in Opioid addiction, is another promising defensive solution against cravings. Since the contents of Alcohol to an Alcoholic releases many euphoric feelings that are similar to those of Opiates (the stone-cold reality of what ethanol does to an Alcoholic is provide them with a trifecta feeling as if taking the numbing and painless proceeds of Heroin, the integrity and boosted confidence of Cocaine and the anxiety-reducing compounds of a Benzodiazepine all methodically wrapped in one), the medical literature has done its best to provide a helping hand accurately for those in need. Not for me. Naltrexone removed all pleasures and aspirations from my daily life, bringing forth the misery of anhedonia. Enjoyable hobbies of mine, like playing guitar and making music, were now performed with lacklustre efforts and sluggish efficacy. Reading books felt mundane. Videos that used to level me with laughter now failed to produce as much as a half-assed smile. After taking Naltrexone for close to a month with failed results, I dispose of the rest of it down the toilet. I'll continue to take Baclofen for the time being. This will work against me in more devilish ways than I can comprehend.

The casket of December is almost at a close. The horizon of 2023 looks slightly more promising than the massacred lands of

2022. It's 8 pm on New Year's Eve. I'm on the way to the liquor store, walking alone along a train track on the east side of town. There's an ineffable eclipse of melancholy coating my path. The Trains that slowly screech past me resemble prehistoric dinosaurs. Monstrous beasts that pay no attention to Human beings. The nighttime mist looks like an emerald swamp has overtaken the sky.

Looking down at my phone, I notice a few notifications from the Dating Application Tinder. Bored and craving a connection with a Female partner, I figure this will help pass the time to enter the New Year and maybe even find a companion as the calendar flips. Due to the importance of this Holiday to be spent with loved ones and social connections, the roads & sidewalks are a graveyard. I feel I'm the only person within 1,000km of this place.

I have a flashback of driving to the Gas Station years ago on Christmas to get more Alcohol. Roads without life. Parking lots & areas that stretch empty for kilometres. This brings me to the outright anguish of being alone with the Reaper. While most are bonding with their family and friends, often I find myself in a two-person party of Alcohol & Me.

I'm in and out of the store in a few blinks of the eye. An Arctic cold Eight-pack of Budweisers are in my grip. Even on the long walk back, I don't drink any of them. I return to my motel room, place them in the fridge and head to sleep.

I'm awoken at 12:01 AM by fireworks and loud cheers down the street by an array of drunk people. I check my phone to see I've matched with a dangerously tempting Redhead girl named Alexandra from the same city. I delete it from my mind, falling immediately back to sleep.

CHAPTER 13

Contagion Mistress

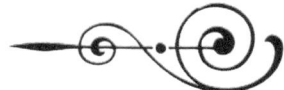

Early-January 2023
Kamloops, B.C., Canada.

W inter has shown up, placing Her hands in mine, saying, "You either fix what is killing you, or you come with me when I leave."

I ignore her.

2023 licks the anvil with its steel fangs and produces a rather flimsy dagger for me to fight these current temptations. The year has changed, but the Weather has refused to follow suit. The job I previously left has allowed me to return to work after a month's absence to clean myself up.

The month I had off was covered under Short-term disability, and I received compensation for the dormant duration. Classified as a Mental Disorder, Alcohol Use Disorder now meets the criteria in the DSM-5 (ALL of these which I gravely have fallen prey to) ;

"DSM-5 criteria are as follows: A maladaptive pattern of substance use leading to clinically significant impairment or distress, as manifested by two or more of the following, occurring at any time in the same 12-month period:

1. Alcohol is often taken in larger amounts or over a longer period than was intended.
2. There is a persistent desire or unsuccessful efforts to cut down or control alcohol use.
3. A great deal of time is spent in activities necessary to obtain alcohol, use alcohol, or recover from its effects.
4. Craving, or a strong desire or urge to use alcohol.
5. Recurrent alcohol use resulting in a failure to fulfill major role obligations at work, school, or home.
6. Continued alcohol use despite having persistent or recurrent social or interpersonal problems caused or exacerbated by the effects of alcohol.
7. Important social, occupational, or recreational activities are given up or reduced because of alcohol use.
8. Recurrent alcohol use in situations in which it is physically hazardous.
9. Alcohol use is continued despite knowledge of having a persistent or recurrent physical or psychological problem that is likely to have been caused or exacerbated by alcohol.

10. Tolerance, as defined by either of the following:

    i.   A need for markedly increased amounts of alcohol to achieve intoxication or desired effect.

    ii.   A markedly diminished effect with continued use of the same amount of alcohol.

11. Withdrawal, as manifested by either of the following:

    i.   The characteristic withdrawal syndrome for alcohol.

    ii.   Alcohol (or a closely related substance, such as a benzodiazepine) is taken to relieve or avoid withdrawal symptoms."

While I'm grateful for social assistance & concrete analytics to support me in such a rambunctious and rough time, this is a touchy subject of *"disease"* versus *"choice"* that often rattles my thoughts. Are Alcoholics who take their right of free will to plunge into decrepitude now granted immunity to the crippling cold frostbite of consequence? Are some too far gone and ride the assisted waves of other's compassion until their last gasps of air? Or are we finally getting to the root cause of addiction, reaping the benefits of all this Scientific discovery inching ever so closely to one grand, defensive solution? Aligned either with affectionate Faith & Hope or the brute force of Tough Love, these angles are open to debate and must be discussed at great length.

The days & nights of the New Year roll on. This past month of cleanliness has only compressed this ferocious and explosive beast inside of me just a few feet below the surface. Like a fully compressed spring the size of a Barn Silo - a few moves and he's sprung loose. None of the medications I'm attached to are working in my favour. Fluvoxamine, Baclofen, Naltrexone - None of these are showing any signs of helpful progress (Fluvoxamine was prescribed to me in March 2021 after I agreed to try another solution to prevent my reoccurring relapses.. in the long run, these pills did more damage creating spiralling and butchering webs of depression that I've never felt before in my life. I absolutely hate taking pharmaceuticals. I always will). Hoping for a guided hand of valour to show me the ways of sobriety in maintenance, these pills facilitate feelings of malaise and provide me more of a reason to reach for a bottle or two (or two hundred).

It takes me nearly two hours to get to work in the morning via city transit. The shop I'm working at requires me to have to transfer between three buses to get to its front doors. The merciless & frigid axe blows of Winter are stiff and agonizing. Not even a few days back on schedule, I started to sip and eventually shotgun cold cans of Kokanee on the bus rides at 6 am. A specific stop in the travels gave me the perfect cover behind a Bus bench to smother the morning's anxieties. I keep a few cans in my backpack at all times. The frost of the outdoors maintains them at a perfect temperature, sometimes near ice. Pairing these with a coffee is a delicate kiss to most of my senses. Though, I am still enraged. I miss having a warm Truck to hop into and make it to my destination in brief periods. The only thing keeping me at this job is the social bonding with one of my coworkers, Cheyenne (she and I will grow closer as friends as life continues to move forward). She capitalizes on hilarity, sharing a very loud and engaging sense of humour, similar to my friends back at home, paired with my typical random antics. Our connection through laughter is key for a productive workday. I don't think I'd want to work here longer than a few weeks without her.

Throughout these remaining weeks before nearing my life's end, into the maggot-infested happenings of the Underworld, I continue to talk with the Redhead I matched on Tinder. My opening pickup line with her was, "If there was a Dating App that matched people via their mental illness compatibility - would you download and use it?"

This worked like black magic in all of the wrong ways. I am playing with the scorching, volcanic heat of an immeasurable amount of danger. I gamble with Death using the magnetizing leashes of sexual attraction to bury all branches of logic. Each interaction with her is catastrophically unsafe for me to continue to wander down, but I continue to do so manically. The alarm bells are rung with bloody limbs; the warning signs are flashing like an epileptic fit of colourful noise puncturing my eye sockets with lava-tipped harpoons. The Fool exposes his jugular to the blade.

She's popular on OnlyFans and brings that upright on the table immediately. Clue number one for the murder scene for this week's forecast. A quasi-gothic/indie princess. A tempting force of nature. In most of her photos, she's dressed in ripped jeans and fishnet tops, covered in jewelry, and her makeup done to the nines. She's dialled in when it comes to a glamorous aesthetic paired with the hippy vibes of a carefree attitude. I've gone down these graven roads before, trying to make something out of this, and moronically, I prepare myself for another beatdown.

A disgusting & slimy grey Friday is heavily breathing against the back of my neck. I'm heading down the road for some lunch during my break at work. A six-pack of Kokanee Beer is rattling about in my Backpack. One of them explodes due to the rumbling of walking downhill. My backpack is soaked with beer and reeks to the high heavens. I've lost a comrade, but knowing there are still five remaining keeps me motivated to find a place to drink. I enter an A&W restaurant and walk into the bathroom, making my way into one of the stalls. This is the ultimate in seclusion for any addict needing to quickly obtain their fix without watching eyes molesting their soul. Still struggling with a bit of *hangxiety* and increased heart rate from the previous night, I take out the beers and start shotgunning them. Liquid wheat transmitting precious feelings of a weightless ascension towards the warm sun. I feel invincible to every single one of life's stressors. The belching from such foamy content is usually a comedy show and a dead giveaway for anyone in the vicinity.

I hike back to work, feeling like I've just accomplished a Worldwide Triathalon Tour, winning Gold, and let the rest of the day be pissed against the wall.

A sea of body-numbing arrows graciously littered me for the remainder of the day due to the alcohol in my bloodstream. Most of the day is spent exchanging messages back and forth with the Redhead from Tinder. Today's day of work was yet again a complete joke due to the poorly managed staff of this company, bloated with cocky & arrogant managers with sore knees due to orally pleasuring the upper echelons. This place is the leading academy for *"How to Become a Laughing Stock with a Cardboard*

Box Degree". All of the other Trucking companies in this town would "talk shit" about this business. I have no idea why I'm working here. The morale of my fellow workers skim the lowest of the low; competence is nowhere to be found. It's a solid paycheck but nothing impressive compared to previous jobs. I exist without purpose and waste most of my time bouncing paycheck to paycheck.

It's time to take myself to task and follow up with these words of seduction I've been playing with all day with Alexandra. I nearly buckle over in a swoon as I stop to embrace the forthcoming attractions. I've mapped out tonight's execution with no attempts to recover from it. I don't press the red button to launch nuclear devastation upon my life lightly with my index finger; I stomp down on it with my size 13 work boot.

After a series of bus rides, overloaded with silvery road slush & the ever so objectionable stench of moist clothing & armpits of other citizens, I make it back to my dimly lit motel room at 6 pm. I purchased a 15-pack of beer on the way home. As I dive into one, I'm reminded of the crackhead living below me who lashes out like a caged Chimp, punching walls and smashing things randomly every other hour that passes. Throughout the day/night, I'll be jolted by thunderous bangs that are sent through the floorboards beneath me. I cannot help but be pissed off that I'm stuck here in a dreary Motel room on a rank side of town. I used to come home to an illuminating and warm household, standing with a beautiful woman & our friendly dog, the views of radiant trees, and the near blinding glistening of the yellow sphere in the sky bouncing off of a crystal lake. The thoughts of the past rub a cheesegrater across my stomach region to and fro with precision and warp speed. The masterful feelings of Wrath promise me a solution—the right direction towards the wrong places. I'm given the power to **choose** whether or not to pull the guillotine rope as I lay helplessly on the bench beneath it. I yank the fibres of string as quickly as it takes for my synapses to process that action.

Alexandra and I throw together some plans so dangerous for me that I may as well have walked naked into a hurricane of razors and expected to have had a better chance of survival. We agree to meet up at one of the many breweries in town. One of the most conniving traits of alcoholism is the ability to hide the problematic strands of its structure from others (for a brief amount of time until it's too late). No one but the Alcoholic who is undergoing the **choice** to enlist in the meticulous madness is aware of its extent. I've told Alexandra little to no statistics about my previous drinking habits, and she seems delighted to connect at the Brewery of our choosing. I fire off a few Snaps to my buddies back home, raving on about how I'm getting to meet this goddess in the flesh. We have a *phone beer* together through a few quick videos of us slamming our drinks doing the full angle swig. After a few more canned suds, I'm out the door and left to advance through the December mist. Each inhale of the Winter vapour reminds me that this superb chemical splendour will come to an end.

The streets of Kamloops during this hour of this Season are scarce of much activity. I pass by a few homeless people decaying amongst blue tarps & cartons of unidentifiable items. The low-wattage streetlamps show little visibility around their camps; it's not like I want to stand and gaze upon them anyway, crouched over in their filth-ridden Zoo. I often wonder if I'll ever get to this level. I'm aware most of these individuals suffer from extreme mental health issues and have signed up to the commitment of ingesting and injecting much more lethal & potent drugs. Alcohol is no different in terms of extremity. It is the elitist sycophant who is given the red carpet and propelled to stardom in this revolting globe of hypocrisy and dysphoria. In my opinion, that makes it far more vicious. It is a long-term investment inviting the Devil into every opportunity you ever have again in your life towards peace and solitude.

I brought a road beer with me, finishing the remnants of it as I arrived at the entrance of the brewing company. One of my co-workers owns & operates this facility with her Husband. In the back of my mind, I have a feeling she'll go easy on me when it comes to settling the bill at the end of the night—more reason for me to go ballistic on the drinks.

Both Alex and I picked the perfect collaborative time to meet one another as we landed on Trivia Night for the shenanigans ahead of us. My co-worker finds me a table at the back of the Bar that gives us a better glimpse of the giant TV screen mounted on the wall. I let her know that I've finally found a date. She laughs in response.

Alex is a little late. I begin to work on a strong cider that pushes a stiff hand of 7% alcohol. The contents overwhelm me. A vortex of serene apples plucked off the trees of Eden, exploding into supernovas you can taste with each sip. These will be my go-to Grenades to consume for the night as I stay focused on a good-tasting ethanol-based attempt at self-immolation. A few minutes pass by. I'm wondering if Alexandra will look as ferociously pleasing as she does in her photos. As I go to drink the last remnants of Cider, I notice Alex walk through the door. I awkwardly raise my arm in the air, motioning toward the table. As she walks forward, I'm given a strong confirmation of her crave-worthy appearance, trying to maintain my casual look without revealing my cupidity. All of the boxes of visual requirements are checked off one by one as I try not to swallow my tongue. Dainty and devilish, she trots up to our table and has a seat across from me. The hue of her eyes resembles Jade Stone being erupted by a miniature pipe bomb of frosty calcite. The symmetry of her jawline connects the dots amongst a newly found celestial constellation reading me tonight's horoscope of good fortunes and aspiring sexual health. She seems so delicate, but she looks like she'd rip me to shreds behind closed doors. I can't tell if I'm smitten with her or floored by being able to consume this much Alcohol and flourish in public again. The carbonated ingredients of my wishing well are overfull, and I'm receiving their requests to blossom into chilled feelings of serenity.

Throughout our night, I learned she had a boyfriend. This internally confuses the hell out of me, but I play along with where I believe this is heading. There are many times in my life when I'll be able to get close to an outrageously attractive female for the sole purpose of being able to hold back and control my sexual advances. I believe they find this more comfortable to be around. I suppose the fine art of *keeping your dick in your pants* pays off when you adhere to the rules of its critical importance.

With no natural awkward pauses throughout the miniature firecrackers we light up together; we seem to hit all the green lights. We end up winning first place in the Trivia Night. That gives us a dorky Trophy and a $100 gift card to come back into this brewery for another round of suicide.

I forget how many Ciders I've conquered in total, but it's somewhere close to seven pints. Alex finishes two or three. Somewhere in between the battlegrounds of alcoholic tug-o-war, we share a few rounds of shots.

Nearing the final hours of the night, Alexandra's boyfriend joins us. While I've remained humble about my own looks in the past, this guy looks like he just woke up outside of a barn. Nowhere could I ever make the connection for these two to be in a relationship? He reminds me of an unintelligent, lazy punk who's using his money and housing situation to hold down this girl. I can't tell if he's intimidated by me. I learned that he was down the road at another bar earlier. His girlfriend has been at a bar with a grown man he knows who is single. How does this make any sense? Are they into Polygamy? Ménage à trois? Free nights out with another to feel up new flesh? Having cast myself as a Monogamist, in the tradition of Romeo, I shrug and keep my face buried in a Cider. Each time it hits my lips, I'm sent a slice of lightning through the creases of my mouth down to my intestines. Each time Alex and I connect pupil to pupil, there's an unexplored, freshly removed bedsheet from the dryer I wish to entangle her with and commit to animalistic tendencies into the night.

We settle the bill. My receipt is usually 90% alcohol and 10% food. That's a concrete staple of my life. I thank my co-worker and tip her generously for serving us the entire night. Again, like a Philanthropist drunk on love, I become an unreasonably high tipper when it's time to hammer down on the debit machine. Tips usually come from my wallet at 45-50% of the total tab. While the degradation of life from Alcoholism is generally a pulverizing array of surgical tools to the Human Body, the generosity of hedonistic spending benefits those who serve the Fool with momentum and efficiency.

Alex and her boyfriend offered to give me a ride back to my motel. I decline the invitation. Alex gives me a back cracker of a hug—such a tight grip for such a small woman. We go our separate ways. I wave goodbye to them as they slip off into the December mist.

The walk home is filled with aggressive tunes of my choice. I'm so ecstatically drunk that I'm screaming lyrics of Limp Bizkit out loud, probably waking up neighbourhoods as I pass by. Headbanging, air guitar, air drums - the whole works to complete the musical experience as if I were on stage or at a show. Sometimes, I get down to my knees on the wet snow, looking towards the sky and shouting with deranged stupidity along with a song. I have flashbacks of my teenage years doing this exact same sequence. In so many ways, I have yet to embrace the open fields towards maturation.

CHAPTER 14

Fractures in the Backbone

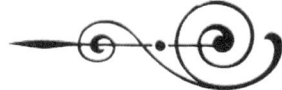

<u>**Mid-January 2023**</u>
<u>**Kamloops, B.C., Canada.**</u>

The hands of time intertwine into a spiral of matrix-like digits, splurging numerical chaos, disrupting one another and unfolding into a new dawn. Last night, I returned to my dismal bachelor pad, a motel filled with my misanthropic pleasures. Empty shells of cans scatter across the wooden floor like a game of Dominos disrupted by a troop of chimpanzees; all sense of order is in disarray. There are no visible or severe mental signs of withdrawal yet. However, an annoying scraping sensation haunts my temples, resembling a deranged knitting needle attempting to reattach the unsettling start of a cranial breach. It's like an elevator that descends only, with no ascent.

The most vulnerable time for an alcoholic is in the hours following a relapse when the burden of guilt becomes overwhelming. What felt like a promising commitment to self-improvement is shattered and pushed underwater until both lungs are flattened. Following my usual pattern after a binge, I lock myself in this motel room for nearly two weeks. The only time I open the door is to accept care packages from a delivery service, which brings bottles of alcohol right to my doorstep. I avoid eye contact as I go to retrieve my paradoxical antidotes, no matter who is at the door. A world-famous celebrity could deliver my lifeline, and I wouldn't even notice. I need that bottle—nothing else.

During these two weeks, my social worker, Madeline, reached out to me several times; her persistent efforts were a reminder of someone who might possibly still care. While my friends and family were doing the same thing, for some disturbing reason, I failed to respond to their pleas. Eventually, I muster the courage to return some of Madeline's messages. She expressed a desire to visit me to check up on my well-being. I felt pretty reluctant at the thought of anyone seeing the chaotic state of my surroundings, a pigsty I had unwittingly allowed myself to become trapped in. I agreed to her visit, hoping for some respite from my current reality.

I still have a troublesome crush on this girl that I can't seem to shake off. Perhaps a long conversation with her could provide clarity, helping me untangle from this concrete bubble wrap, each pocket filled with maiming nails. She tells me she'll be over in an hour. Is that a sufficient amount of time to pull myself together and become presentable, adhering to the respectable basics of chivalry? I use this time to drink more.

The swigs of this clear pesticide continue.

A brief knock evolves around my front door frame. I peek through the eyehole and see Madeline standing with another girl. I can't tell if I'm being blinded by the piercing frost and snow outside or the grace of seeing Madeline up close again. Letting them inside, I walk back to my kitchen and sit against the fridge door. The dining room is doused with bottles, articles of clothing, upside-down cartons of pop, packages of unopened food containers, bottles of cologne, pill capsules, books, my bicycle and some random supplement jars. Before they walk in, I spray the room with one of the cologne bottles to pathetically try and mask any scent of this hellhole. The looks on the two girl's faces are of discomfort but acceptance.

Madeline is wearing a tan-coloured toque and dressed in the typical Canadian winter clothing, which maximizes her glamour. Her vivid tropical blue eyes are sources of ethereal sparkle that could recharge any room concealed with darkness.

A temporary state of alleviation exists when I'm speaking with her. I barely recognize or notice her friend. Our conversations are relatively buoyant; that is until I'm hit by drunken cockiness and a throatful of regret. In my broken speech patterns, I moronically tell her I found her on Facebook and am envious of her boyfriend. While things have been amicable between us for the last month or so, my choice of words garner all the ounces of stupidity I have to offer her and are dropped heavily on her lap. Her face goes a little sour, and there's an awkward break in the room. From here, the stupor mutates into fragments. Maybe it was the unbelievably deathly swig of Vodka I took before they walked into my room, but I lose touch with reality. Portions of my memory fly by me as I'm voluntarily smashing my head into the wall of my dining room. I remember having a machete in my hand and a can of bear mace in the other. I see a ripped blanket on the ground. I can smell the winter frost dancing outside the walls and the stale decay of the porcelain tub in the bathroom. Maddie and her friend come and go.

Suddenly, I'm in handcuffs and in the back of a cop car. My head is against my knees. Reality starts to wisp its way back to my vision. I'm aware I didn't do anything to Madeline or her friend. Maybe I started talking about some of the violent ideas I have against hateful Men and those who have bothered me in my life. Perhaps I put Death Metal on full blast and was going over some of the lyrics with them, or began to dissect some of the most disturbing poems and lyrics I've ever written. I probably scared the shit out of them, and they called the police on me. I am extremely vigilant in my belief that I did not cause them any harm. The police officer confirms this. Again, my spastic weaving in and out of a stupor continues.

"You posed a risk to yourself," the officer interjects as we glide through the snow toward our unknown destination, "we just want to prevent anything terrible from happening."

I respond, "I've never committed to any acts of self-harm. I'm not suicidal."

The officer comes back with, "Do you believe what you're doing to yourself is not an act of self-harm? I've never seen so many alcohol bottles in a single room."

I'm still drunk out of my mind, but those words resonate and settle in the bottom of my guts.

Without a clue of where we're headed, I begin to picture the worst. Maybe they're finally going to toss me in prison or some other sanitarium filled to the brim with psychotics and negatively functioning schizophrenics. My alcohol use is bringing all of those forms of mental illness to my household. Maybe I belong there.

I recognize the surrounding view as we pull up to the Royal Inland Hospital in Kamloops. Still in handcuffs, I'm led into a dark room in some mystery area of the hospital.

I am forever walking the opposite way towards paradise.

Being ushered into another main room with a hospital bed, I'm finally free of the hand chains. I notice Madeline and another worker talking outside in the hallway. I apologize and assure the staff that I am not a danger to myself. I simply consumed too much alcohol and made a foolish choice to seek attention by being dramatic. Though they remind me I need not apologize, they are doing their best to fast-track me to a spot in Detox. This usually takes two to three weeks, but with the help of Madeline and a few others, they're able to secure me a bed in a few days. In the back of my mind, the perversion of this insanity is ecstatic to understand I don't have to entirely give up drinking just yet. I have a feeling I'll be let go soon.

I meet with a counsellor before I'm discharged. He's a tall and burly gentleman who is easy to get along with, promising me that this deception will end soon. I save his number in my phone, thank him profusely, and tell him I will contact him once this is over. I completely forget who he is as soon as I leave the room.

With three days to transpire before Detox, I promise to dial back a little bit on the alcohol distortion knob. Instead, I commit to the solid beers and pick up a 15-pack of Colt 45s on my way back to the motel room. During the walk back, I'm well aware of the decadence surrounding me. Gone are the days of self-tenderness and flowering aspirations. The following days will be tattooed with pitiful guilt and deathly nihilism.

I've stayed true to my word and kept it to strong beers. I'm able to do a little more around my room and get around town when consuming just beer. I use this to fuel my habit. While the philosophy seems reasonable when compared to my history of the devastation caused by hard alcohol, the number of beers I'm able to drink is a complete fucking gong show and proves to be just as problematic. I'm able to closely reach the same levels of intoxication with 8% beers that go down like purified water. Whether it be beer or spirits, both cause loss, both cause hardships - both are imposters pretending to be your buddy until you've finally been granted a certificate of DOA.

I get a text from Madeline.

She says, "Are you ready to go to Detox today?"

I reply, "You better believe it… Let's do this."

She fires back, "Okay. I'll be there in 45 minutes. See you soon."

Does it all cease to exist today? No more parties of camaraderie with every human being I meet from here on out. No more extravagant socializing with a full glass in hand, believing the contents of it all will bring hopeful interactions with others, but most importantly, there will be no more covering for my inadequacies of ever having to face who I genuinely am once sober.

"I'm here," Madeline's name flashes on my phone.

Again, I've packed nothing for what should be a seven-day stay at this Detox Facility. I bring some facewash, some underwear, and deodorant, and that's about it. I slam two beers and put another one in my pocket before leaving the motel room. Madie's white SUV is in the parking lot below me. Her friend is in the passenger seat.

I hop into the backseat, closing the door lightly beside me.

"So," Madeline cutely says, "are you excited for this?"

"You have no idea," I respond.

In reality, I'm the one who has no idea. I can't tell if I'm ready to give this all up. Booze has taken virtually every last entity of a worthwhile life from me. Fields of colourfully lit flowers ripped and raped from root to tip. The cliche rings in my head; I've lost my house, career, girlfriend, friends, passions, investments, finances, strength, and life from all of this... and I still don't want to quit. The realization of such ruination is crippling.

I pull out the beer I brought along with me and ask Madeline if I can drink it in the car since it may be one of the last ones I ever have the dishonour of consuming. She tells me to wait until we get outside the detox centre.

On the drive over, I show both of them the music I've recorded and created over the last year and a half. I figure this would be a time to boast a little of my musical talents to a girl I still hold infatuation for.

The three of us are now parked outside of the Detox clinic. We take a final moment to listen to one of my acoustic tracks. I crack the beer I brought and sip it like it's the last bottle of water on earth, and I'm about to go on an exhibition across the middle regions of the Australian deserts.

Madeline and her coworker look generally impressed by a few of my songs, ranging from my acoustic folk ballads or melancholic piano pieces. I can't tell if they're just saying that because I'm in their presence, but I can feel them genuinely being honest about it. It's a warming feeling to take with me as I say my goodbyes and crush this final beverage of malt liquor.

Thanking them for the ride across town, I collect my belongings and march forward to where I will almost lose my life in the days to come.

CHAPTER 15

Amythest Lacerations

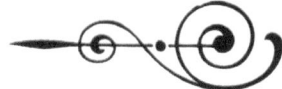

<u>Late-January 2023</u>
<u>Kamloops, B.C, Canada</u>

Miniature pyramids of snow crunch under my Converse shoes as I lean down to have a seat outside of a detox clinic located in the lower intestinal region of Kamloops. I'm holding the book *"All the Light We Cannot See"* in front of me, painfully squinting due to the strong pearl glimmers of this January atmosphere. I found this book earlier in the tiny library inside of the living quarters, figuring it would be best to occupy my mind with a new story while undergoing these unsung events. I'm at an incomprehensible beginning stage of entering an unknown landscape of delusions, false beliefs, and hallucinations. Of course, unbeknownst to me, I'm entirely aloof and detached from being able to do anything about it.

At this moment, I haven't had a drink of alcohol for over 48 hours. I haven't slept either. I'm not sure if the Nurses here have properly been allowing me to continue to take the Baclofen that I've been on for just about two months (which was prescribed at this very facility) and the Fluvoxamine I've been taking for well over a year and a half. Not only is my brain undergoing the absence of alcohol (which I have been given Phenobarbital to wade off withdrawal symptoms), but it is also receiving heavy blows from the absence of these other medications that have been brought upon me via doctor's recommendations. The pills I'm taking morning, day and night don't resemble the regular supplements & medications I've been on these last 60 days. Nothing feels right, but for the most bizarre reason that I can't seem to describe entirely, the option of panicking feels suppressed. My anxiety has vanished, but I'm feeling like paranormal holes are filling my body with venom. An unknown, unobservable entity is looming just behind me. I can feel it with every registering sense left that's working in my body, but I can't do anything about it. The play button is pressed, and I'm puppeteered along for the ride.

As I'm flipping pages throughout the book in my hands, trying my best to spend any sort of focus on this activity, I notice a dark figure standing beside one of the trees a few metres ahead of me. The figure reveals itself to be a cute brunette-haired woman. Feeling like she's been watching me for a few minutes, I stand up and try to talk to her. She doesn't respond. As I walk forward to formulate a greeting, she hides behind another tree. Prickles of pine needles leap off the tree branch to the snow below.

The hum of helicopters buzzes overhead like incognito honeybees in search of dying crops. I get closer to the second tree the woman is hiding behind. I can clearly see her standing beside it, her hair hanging down, swaying slightly in the wind. Moving closer to the timber, no one is to be found. I do a quick 360 and analyze all paths around me. The unidentified woman appears to have never been there. Did she become absorbed into the tree bark? Was that a servant of Mother Nature trying to warn me of this approaching hellish overthrow? Before I can try to strip the tree of its earthly skin, I notice another figure, about 50 metres ahead of me, leaning against the wall and having a cigarette. My viewpoint is looking up from the bottom of the facility towards the large hill towards the West. The overcast sky looks like it is slitting its own throat, spewing gray water from its cut wounds into decomposing clouds, ragged and being drained of life. From this distance, the manly figure appears to be one of the guys I befriended inside the common hall. There are roughly 20 other people in here with me, all varying from ages 18 to 65. I put my hand up to wave to him as he puffs from his cancer stick. I begin to walk through the snow, looking to have a conversation with him to ask if he's seen a brown-haired woman pass by here. Each small step towards him causes his body to move away from my presence as if almost shape-shifting.

I stop in my tracks to calculate all in front of me.

The aura of this granite Winter swims from North to South, East to West. I feel every object in front of my eyes turn to stone and then back to life. The figure of the Man, who I had just seen physically moving and looking towards me, fades into the surface he was leaning on. I'm distracted by the images on the wall he slipped into. Painted on the wall is a mural of Three friendly-looking Brown Bears conversing with each other. The longer I look at the Bears, the more sinister they become. Their gleeful smiles become twisted into a cultish demonic outburst of horror. My body is trying to scream out for help, but something is weighing it down. Something is smothering it with a back-breaking blanket of silence. I'm left standing in the rotting snow, looking out towards the city lights, utterly bare of life.

Collecting my array of thoughts, I head back inside to my room to warm up.

The minute I make it to my bunk, my nose starts to bleed.. badly. I'm able to slow it down by sitting against a wall in the hallway with a rag to my nose. A nurse walks by and asks if I'm doing alright. I agree that I've had a few of these moments with nosebleeds as a kid—nothing to worry about. On top of all of these ghastly symptoms of evident progression toward Delirium Tremens, my speech has become heavily slurred. Even though I am noticing this, what is happening in my brain prevents me from responding to the severity. Formulating a complete sentence takes me a few seconds, and the words are broken as if I am suffering from an impediment of sorts. When I call my friends and family from the payphone on the wall, it takes everything for me to try and connect the dots of my personal linguistic system together. I can register their voices and speech just fine, but I'm having desperate trouble with my own. Was I about to have a stroke? The nurses on shift take notice of it.

Each one of my steps now has my feet feeling like I've equipped bowling balls for shoes. They're heavy and misguided. My positioning feels off balance and there is an apparent gait in my walk. These are all involved in the list of ailments I've acquired in these first few days at Detox. The Staff do little to provide me with proper grounds for healing and safety while staying there. I should have immediately been taken to the hospital the moment all of these disorders unveiled themselves at once. These are stark warning signs of incoming Delirium Tremens, which brings about a chance of death. I'm coherent enough not to raise the alarms of my rocketing decline.

As I walk back to my room, I meet a dark-haired woman in the hallway who says she brought me some comfy track pants to wear at night. She was carrying with her a gray bin of clothing and said she'd be back in my room later to hand them to me. She walks off to the end of the hallway into the darkness. I forgot to grab her name. I double-checked with a Nurse to ask about the identity of who she was. I'm told nobody like that exists at this facility. With precise detail, I hammer my point across to the nurse, saying that I had just physically seen this individual a few minutes ago. Her presence was more accurate than the changing of seasons. Nobody does anything about it. I'm at a desperate and complicated mental loss. I retire to my bedroom.

The Moon has taken command in the faint sky. I've been awake for almost three days. The lack of alcohol in my system sends my mind & body into a state of half-paralyzed shock. My nerves are chilled with the administration of Phenobarbital, but I can still feel the endings of them wishing to evacuate at any chance they get. Like a helpless piece of trash that's left to spin wildly in the wind, dancing with itself in a vacant Parking lot, I go with the flow of this facility, believing they're doing all they can to provide me safe treatment for coming off of Alcohol.

Even heavily medicated, I fail to ascend into a proper dream world and fail to begin my road to healing. There are no more chances left to stir about in this quiet room of soon-to-be horrors. All paths are manned by disfigured gargoyles armed with pitchforks, maces, two-handed cleavers, and other piercing forms of weaponry. I am a frail man approaching the gates of Hell wearing only torn rags to protect my skin from the embers. A life raft has been thrown three feet too far away for me to reach as I'm birthed into a dark Ocean of limb-removing waves.

At this point, I have little idea of who or what is guiding me around this physical plane of existence. I feel like a character in the video game "The Sims" being toyed with and sent all around the room in different directions. With possibly the last coherent and functional thought-to-action response my brain will conjure, I stumble out of my room towards the nurse's office to ask for anything they can do to help me sleep. I'm tired of gazing at the roof, losing track of whether my eyes are open or closed. I can no longer tolerate the sound of music humming & breathing through the walls at random frequencies and pitches. I'm on my knees on train tracks, with my hands to the sky, waiting to collect the feverish formula of how quickly my bones break from the force of a freight train.

The medical staff agreed to try an injection of Haloperidol, an antipsychotic medication commonly used for Schizophrenics/

people suffering from hallucinations. None of my mental functioning resembles being Human anymore, so I agree and aimlessly fall back into my bedroom. The nurse follows me and readies the drugs. This is part of the few remaining physical visions I'll have of being on Earth. The nurse uses a large needle to inject Haloperidol intramuscularly into the upper region of my left arm. There wasn't any deep inhaling or preparing myself for the injection; it just happened. We both silently agree that this should rescue me from the endless suffering of the inferno of insomnia. However, this was just me submitting to the creatures below, filing their claws with tools like a thin peasant from the Medieval ages. The nurse leaves the room and closes the door. I'm hoping this remedy will shelter me from the swords raining from the sky.

Fifteen minutes goes by, maybe twenty. All the walls breathe a murderous deep blue mixed with a bubbling froth of yellow urine. There are enough Ants on the floor to fill the back of a dump truck. They're all squeaking and shining, rolling together like a Royal Rumble of contenders on Wrestlemania. Each one of them has a white glowing speck on the crowns of their heads. How I can see this is beyond me. As I reach to turn the lamp off that's beside me, I'm unaware that the second I turn off the lights is when I will grant myself access to a new plane somewhere other than this planet. The flick of the switch is the process of descension to the abyss, which has been written about for centuries in ancient texts. Perhaps it was the invitations penned in the blood that I shot down towards the pit of brimstone, down a cataclysmic tube held together by Human skin. They answered the call; this room was now a Portal to and from Hell.

The alarm clock across the room beams its crimson projection to the roof. It looks like glowing lava underneath a dark sea with Eels and oceanic creatures swimming by it. I can't tell if suddenly I've been thrown underwater with breathing apparatus to witness such sights. I feel as if I'm swimming in a vat of fat grease, eyes wide open and burning. An eclipse of the Moon appears on the walls. I'm witnessing this for the first time in my life while submerged in the luminescent brutality of every horrendous dark colour that is known to Man.

I'm thrown back to being at my bedside. Suddenly, the extension cord of the alarm clock is sucked into the wall like a murderously strong vacuum has been activated, being sent up to the roof as if God were playing Tug-O-War with it and sent back down to the floor in the blink of an eye. There's a sublime demonic presence behind the walls, losing its mind. The clock goes with it and has disappeared entirely. Whatever is happening, it is terrifying to know that it has taken away the measure of time and agency for me to follow. Time no longer exists. My first reaction is mere acceptance. I don't lash out in fear of what is going on. I take things rather slowly and survey the room for all that is transpiring. I turn the lamp back on to better glimpse my surroundings.

As the light penetrates the churning black web of this departure into a Sea of delusion, all around me multiplies the madness. I sit straight up from my bed. I look down at my hands, noticing I'm holding some bizarre silver candy bar wrapper that looks like a compressed cinder block. I feel it for its concrete texture, but as I motion to touch it with my other hand, it morphs into a longer piece of silver that now resembles one of a wet napkin package. There are hieroglyphics and unintelligible writing up and down the silver coating of the wrapper. Like exploring the backdrop of a deep cave that was created 8,000 years ago - occultist symbols and strange characters levitate off of it. I notice the ends are serrated and can be torn open. Without much hesitation, I tear open the package with excitement like I used to with Pokemon Cards back in the late 90's. Stardust pours out of the rip in the silver wrapper, which has now adapted to a more glowing colour of Grey.

Before I can make much sense of it, a Bee, roughly two inches in length, flies out of it. Each second, it changes from a wasp to a miniature floating fairy, to an indescribable piece of plastic that resembles a suction cup, and back to a hornet. It lands on the cupboard across the room and begins speaking to me in a robotic voice. It's here to help (or so it says). It's coated in gelatinous embryonic fluid. Out of nowhere, I'm ignited with feelings of pure hostility. My life depends on making sure whatever this thing is murdered. There is zero trust here. However, there is this lustrous enchantment of illusionary confusion. How does the mind produce such a vision? When the fairy speaks, it hauntingly provides me with random world news and methods of how bones heal when they break. It seems lovely, though malicious and devilish. Like paying close attention to the ramblings of a Schizophrenic, these circumstances make little sense. My mind races like two mass murderers put into a room with an innocent person tied to a lone chair.

The colours in the room shift their brightness & contrast settings as if fumbling with their own TV remote in a panic to escape from the settings menu. I'm honed in on trying to understand where this ever-transforming Insect has come from and why it's talking to me. It has flown across the room and is now hiding between the seams of the window to the outside world. I can barely see its head just protruding out of the glass, but it's incredibly terrifying and providing me with an ineffable threat to my life. As calm and calculated as it sounds, its presence is beyond the concept of danger. I do my best to try and butcher it. I forge on to obliterate its existence.

This entire time, it was softly chanting the Canadian Anthem and would briefly pause to tell updates of Israelian and Palestinian combat. It keeps poking its bleeding head out of the glass, making agonizing noises of random bleeps and trying to find a proper radio station, spinning the frequency knob around and around. I've had enough of this parasite interfering with my night. I grab one of my books off of the table beside me and whip it across the room towards the creature. It misses by a few feet. The noise continues. During all of this, the ants keep rank and file going on strong in the background. The defiling flow of their pinchers, their slimy legs making all around squirm. Thousands of them filtrating through the walls and floors. One by one, adhering to their patriotic system.

I stand up and jolt across the room, avoiding the ants, clutching the book with both hands and smashing down onto the exposed head of this unknown insect. Like a game of whack-a-mole, the insect's head appears and I come smashing down. That worthless feeling that your best offence is a book. I use coercion and vocal strategy to make the soft-voiced creature reappear when I miss. Piece by piece, sections of its head are torn off as I use the book as a dissecting device. Eventually, just a sliver of its body is remaining. It has fallen in between the window sill and the glass. I can still hear it screaming. I remove the cover of the book, sliding its thinness between the glass, and hear the final crunches of the creature's body being squished. It's dead. I've murdered some sort of spawned demonic entity.

I can't even throw my arms in the air for a victory dance before the actual incisions into other realms & planes begin to stretch and break open. Upon killing this nameless insect, a fairy appears a couple of feet in front of my eyes. Cosmic space dust twinkles behind each of its strides in the air. I try to reach for it, but it floats to the roof and vanishes. As I lower my head to view outside the window, there's clear visual evidence that I'm shifting away from the physical realm.

Outside, I notice one of my friends and two other unknown people standing beside a large cedar tree. The three of them are pointing and laughing in my direction. The silhouettes of their structures buzzing and humming like a 9.9 magnitude earthquake is happening outside. Was this all a sick joke? Was there a plan all along? My friend's face hangs down by at least three feet, looking like someone had managed to wedge a pumpkin inside of their mouth & mercilessly down their throat. The trees and plants behind them are all glowing, dark and deep. Organ matter seems to connect each one via strands of DNA-linked codes not known to humanity. One would never know that dark can glow. The cedar is like a removed, fresh ribcage.

I am briefly aware of this vicious mental game of barbed wire. I feel the trouble boiling on the horizon, but the feeling of understanding fails to grasp me. I look down and notice that my palms have been hacked at, like going wrist-deep into a bowl of Piranhas. Gauze wrapped up so bloody bright red that it would catch the attention of a thirsty Bull kilometres away. Elements of physicality no longer apply. The three previously mentioned figures of my friend and her two shadow figures are inhaled into the black diamond clouds above. The outside apocalypse smoulders. If Picasso could paint this scene, there would be no sum of money to put a value on such inconceivably rich explosions of such stimulation.

I'm ripped away from the facade of beauty outside. Footsteps and chaos spin above me all about. I can hear the voices of my Sister and her best friend clambering about on the roof. I haven't seen either of them for far too long. I miss speaking with my Sister. There's a brief injection of hope that I will get to talk to her. Even though I'm aware of my situation, at the same time, I'm entirely unaware. I can do nothing but allow this game to unravel and fall with the notion of sporadic change.

I hear them making a slow walk toward the other side of the building. I follow their footsteps, walking each time that they do, towards the door of my room. Oddly enough, the mutations of ants around the room have all disappeared. I make it to my door and fling it open. A blast of the hallway lights reminds me that this place still exists in the realm of practicality. It is here that I make my final few steps towards the uncharted mountainous pathways to Hell. The second I leave my room, I lose consciousness. The world of the fatefully mystical and metaphysical swallows me whole.

CHAPTER 16

Being Beheaded in Hell

I am a passerby witnessing unrestrained violence, walking directionless on the cliffsides of maroon brimstone. Bizzare and brutish bald creatures are ripping their skin off in small pieces while they decimate other Men in their grasp. If it can bleed - the lacerations are a must. They squeeze corpses in rages of a psychotic obsession. The mush of skin explodes in their wiry fingers. There's no screaming but, instead, graphically horrendous smacking sounds of blood and eyeballs being crushed together continuously. There's no stopping. Chokeholds are applied to their throats. Abdominal regions are erupting like waves of Rose Quartz and Rubies are strapping themselves with dynamite and committing suicide. Repeatedly. The blows are sending slaughtering waves of masochistic bludgeoning in all directions. Bodies are bent backwards, and the regions of their spinal columns are split through their stomachs, leaving rows of vertebrae skimming off the ground that are coated with bodily fluids. There is a disturbing feeling of arousal in the air. All there is to drink is gasoline. These beasts are having an extravagant buffet on an exuberant massacre of guts. Dripping copper cliffs are doused with grains of sand. Salt that would typically disinfect & mend wounds is now used to suffocate all airways toward any working pairs of lungs in this abyss. The weather forecast here predicts an eternity of solar flares eating each millimetre of working muscle fibres with a permanently active flamethrower. There are winding pathways that lead to uninhabited islands to nowhere. Perhaps there are more caves and passages of facesplitting torture. While I have noted that time does not exist here, I'm thankfully only shown this area for what felt like a brief period.

Darkness.

I'm thrown face-first to the floor of the inside of a city bus barrelling down an imageless road. No city lights or symbols, except for the concrete outside, exist on this gaping black hole of a globe. Surrounding me are thick-coated Men of all shapes and sizes. An eerie and penetrating deep blue of their skin sends alerting waves with whatever I have left on my body to receive signals with. I have no clue if I have limbs on my body until I look down and get a grip on where I'm at. No coordinates are available to properly provide a position where I'm standing. Numbers self-destruct and lose all meaning.

I notice one of these assailants about to strike me across the shoulder with something. I grab a hold of the cylindrical object being used to break my neck. I slam it forward towards whoever this son of a bitch is. As I move in to try and choke the Man with his weapon, his face appears in a stream of vomit-inducing colours. Livid facial expressions of a psychopathic & demonic clown stretch all around as if it were possible for a Human Face to be injected with helium, just reaching the point of erupting. None of the other Men are doing anything. All I'm focused on is trying to kill this thug, this complete piece of shit. Today's sacrifice will be this worthless heap of organs. I wish to floss my teeth with his bones once this is over. I have never been so amped by such a devastating revocation of someone's life.

It takes forever to end this Man. I've smashed the window beside us open with my bare fists. I drag the back of his head across the sharp pieces of busted glass still stuck in the bottom of the window. Hair and chunks of flesh are caught between each of my fingers. So much bubbling thick goo is caked to my hands like quick-drying adhesive. The roof lights flicker like a panicked heartbeat. The stop-and-go of light helps me get an assessment of the relentless amount of gore around me. All of the surrounding men transform into heaps of rotting skin. Nothing phases me. Both of my feet are now on this Man's throat. I see his teeth breaking through his lips, spitting blood and unknown juices towards the roof of the bus. I crank my foot up like pulling a motor to life and begin stomping a hole through the top of his head. Sparks shoot out of his throat and where my foot meets his skull. His entire face is almost flattened to the symmetry of the floor. I still hear him breathing. He just won't die. I see his smushed eyeballs somehow moving back and forth; his teeth spilled all over the place. I'm being dragged off the bus by random vines and large hands. The bus has ended its tour of the sightless gutters. We are now stopped on a river of glass. The fighting stops. The front of the bus door opens, and at the same time, my mind and vision split into halves.

Darkness.

Paralyzed and trapped in a basement with a few other shadow figure stragglers, my limbs are comatose, but I still feel awake. I'm weighed down on a large mattress with two other unknown bodies to my left and right. We wither away in the dark and try to break free of our chains. Nothing works. With all of the strength I can manage, I try sitting up. Nothing works. I notice two doors a dozen feet away from me brightly lit up. In these other rooms are various groups of old high school friend lookalikes. One-half of the group is gaming on computers; the other half is playing cards. They peer into the room every other minute to see if I'm still attached to my leash/chains. I can hear myself weeping at the thought of being chained to two corpses that now look like they are having grand mal seizures. The body to my right loses its arms and legs. A torso is now dangling and dancing in chains. A miniature comet shoots across the roof, lighting up the ground that I lay on. The scent of freshly dug soil waltzes around this mysterious crypt. It looks like I'm floating in midair. There is no ground, no floor, no pavement. Around me is a spherical void of unending patterns and shapes. Winded by an unperceived infiltration of every last neurotransmitter throughout the workings of my brain, the power of belief returns to me; there still remains to be an *I*. With this, I am brought into the drilling hands of Death. Is this my final vision before the void takes me with it? Does this mean I have another chance somewhere else? Both of the doors I saw earlier appear closer together than last time and slam shut.

Cosmic blue. Crystals torn to shreds. Glossy and pearl Diamonds spew from a volcano. Electrified shrapnel. Shells of Obsidian atoms are split along with Uranium and Plutonium holding their hands.

I'm transferred back to the tangible world.

CHAPTER 17

Charcoal Slivers

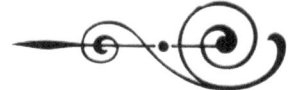

Dimly lit hospital room lights pump their aura back into my perception. Both of my arms and legs are restrained to a gurney. My sensory faculty starts to breathe oxygen found on this Earth once again. I could have sworn I was just in an underground bunker, ready to unhinge my arms from a stronghold of chains. Where did I go? What happened to me? The relief of being able to process my previous sentiments opens a gate of brief inquisition. A nurse comes in and loosens the straps found around my ligaments. I swear I've seen her before. I ask if we've ever crossed paths at a time in our past. As she disagrees, she removes a towel that's around my groin region and leaves the room. With heavy and nearly closed eyes, I stare around the room in disbelief at the concept of reality.

Small portals still open and close around me. I notice a deliciously bright red can of Coca-Cola resting on the side of a table across the room with a tightly wrapped sandwich that looks like it was freshly prepared in the kitchen of a 5-star elite restaurant. I groggily rise from the bed, taking off the loose straps found around my body. As I stretch toward the can of Coke and the tempting stack of bread, they vanish. Blinking as if all of this is still a normal occurrence, I lay back down and return to my period of self-questioning. I look to my right to a table that's much closer to me than the previous one. Again, a sweating can of Cola marked with cold water drops is on it, right in front of me, within reach. I pick it up. I can physically feel this carbonated beverage and the cold properties of its aluminum exterior. The sensation of its internal fizz couldn't be more real. I go to open it up, and it disappears. I'm left to stare at my open hands.

The surrounding curtains of privacy are swaying slowly from side to side from what appears to be a draft from the roof ventilation. They remind me of the rundown bathroom sheets I had hanging in my old motel room. My awareness is returning like a bipolar boomerang. I look past the curtains and see a familiar face watching me from the hallway. It's my social worker, Madeline. She waves to me when we make eye contact. Is she real? How do I recognize that this is actually her? Were our interactions of a few months ago even a reality? Or have I been swimming in a hallucinatory cascade of transcendence and other dimensions for the last three months? Five months? As these questions mass multiply, they're also executed the moment I finish asking them. My brain is rapidly repairing itself and grounding toward a fortified sensibility. No answers are becoming concrete until a Doctor appears through the curtains and softly speaks to me.

"Jordan," she says calmly, "make sure to call your family as soon as you can. Use this to reach them." She hands me a cordless phone. After all that I've just been decimated with, I still remember my Mom's phone number. A positive green checkmark that my memory has not been tampered with and that brain damage has been avoided (for all I hope to believe).

The conversation is brief, but I'm able to tell her that I'm alive. I probe for questions as much as I can. My Mom isn't quite able to tell me what happened, as she's located four hours away and was (thankfully) not here to witness this deathly excursion, but from what I'm translating, it sounds like I've just undergone a severe case of Delirium Tremens, being placed in a drug-induced coma for over 48 hours. I'm at a loss for words and still trying to comprehend the visions and areas I returned from. I can still see and feel the warm charcoal rub marks on my hands from the horrific and barbarous arena of brimstone. Observing the clock on the hospital wall brings back my awareness of time, and healing from this will require a significant amount of it. Through the healing comes deeply harvested learning and, from there, the expression of cultivated truth.

After such an overflux of otherworldly motivations, my beliefs and perception of reality have forever changed. Being shown the outstretched views into a massively unexplored universe of wherever the principal destination of this current life goes after it's depleted, whether this be a subjective world or not, entangles the 3.3 pounds of jelly between the confines of my skull with numbing curiosity. Each moment of deja vu, second-guessing, or pondering reality is forever marked with an ominous mystery that something else may be flourishing in other realms. Near-death experiences jampack an inconceivable amount of stimulation amongst the psyche that something rips the wrapping paper off of a concealed portal to shreds, revealing the gifts of infinite grandeur or endless paradoxical energy.

CHAPTER 18

Last of the Forest Embers

In the following months, distressingly enough, even after crawling in the filth of Death with both of my eyes sloppily stitched closed, I relapsed twice more, unable to silence the lure of the harmonies coming out of the bottle, playing so beautifully in an orchestrated magnetization. Amongst the carnage, I'm still able to write, record, and release more music (some being my personal favourites), hauling my laptop, guitar and keyboard around with me wherever I manage to find work.

Shortly after being released from the hospital in January, I found employment in the city of Williams Lake at a largely successful corporate trucking company. Thrown halfway up the province of British Columbia, my only legal way of transportation is via E-Bus. Walking to and from work calculates close to 10km every day & night.

I've booked a month's stay at an Air BnB to allow me enough time to get my living situation sorted out. I have to leave an hour and a half early to make it to work on time. Though visually beautiful from the icy serene fields and snow-packed forests, the crisscross mountains & frozen lakes, travelling by foot in the -20 & -30 winters was miserable and risky due to being exposed to the wildlife. I equipped myself with a small knife and some mace, but I have no clue if that would have done much damage to some of the Cougars here in the interior of B.C.

The laces on my work boots are pulled tight. I can only hope I don't run into any bears along the way.

A guy I work with eventually offers to give me lifts in the morning & after work.

Still with no driver's license and no battle plan to try and survive the Winter, right as I got my local gym membership and was feeling relatively stable, my tolerance for a sober life lasted a mere three weeks before I snapped and ventured into a Brewing company, meeting a waitress who I had matched on a dating app the previous night. We get blitzed up, and just like any other moment where I have tried to manage one night of drinking responsibly, all hell breaks loose, and I'm found in handcuffs in less than seven days.

One of my close friends from the Lower Mainland, Grace, calls law enforcement to do a wellness check on me. All things considered, she does me a great favour in bringing a dose of authority to my rambunctious behaviour. I've known her and the rest of her family for over 14 years, usually conversing on any other terms than this. The neck-breaking plume of embarrassment is challenging to comprehend.

In the back of the police cruiser, I text my boss and tell him I'm no longer able to work for them—another employment opportunity executed like useless cannon fodder.

I'm released later on in the day.

Having to trek from Williams Lake back to Abbotsford (over 500km south) without a car (while belligerently intoxicated), hauling around every article of clothing and instrument that I own in large travel bags is next to impossible.

I managed to book another E-Bus.

On this ill-fated departure, I make it to the halfway checkpoint in Kamloops while waiting for the next bus heading south to arrive.

As I exited the bus, in some sort of drunken blinding haze, I stumbled towards an open pub that was connected to the bus station. Gunned beyond comprehension, I put my Acoustic guitar down at the front entrance of the bar.

Knowing I have more alcohol in my backpack and don't need to spend any more at the bar, I walk off back to the bus station, forgetting that I've left my musical instrument behind.

A couple of minutes pass, and the absence of my guitar finally sinks in.

Thinking my guitar has been stolen alerts every defensive mechanism that's still awake in my body with morbid malice. I jump to conclusions and run into the nearby security office, screaming, asking them to review the cameras to see if someone has run off with my prized musical possession.

The security guard is easily persuaded.

We go over the surveillance tape and see my stumbling corpse appear beneath the camera, placing my guitar down and aimlessly walking off. The Guitar still rests there in its case. I'm so goddamn annihilated from the alcohol that I forget where I've put one of the most essential objects I'll ever possess in my life.

The security guard looks over at me awkwardly, starting to take in how removed from reality I am. From here, he alerts the staff of the E-Bus.

A cocky suit-wearing prick marches out of his office and tries to usher me out the door, being upfront and forceful as I previously caused quite a commotion.

As more security guards are added to the mix, trying to get me outside, I notice a tire iron in one of my travel bags. Grabbing it with murder in my eyes, I threaten the suit-wearing guy. It's not my most brilliant move when surrounded by a plethora of enforcement. None of these guys are Police Officers, so a mismatched game of no progress goes to a stalemate. As they go to call the Cops, I desperately grab every bag (most notably my Guitar) and run outside, down a few blocks, until I collapse on the ground with my belongings.

I'm gazing up at the putrid gray marble-top sky. I feel like puking, crying, laughing and ejaculating all at the same time. A howitzer of hysteria and mania is swallowing me alive.

Trapped in the lumbering city of Kamloops, once again, I make a call for help to my friend Cheyenne, who comes to my rescue. I am highly grateful for her, as she has rescued me from a few situations when I lacked a logical exit strategy. Her demeanour is always calm and understanding, and I am reciprocal and treat her the same way.

She allows me to stay at her house for one night. We order Chinese food, and I spend most of the night drunkenly talking to her cat, eventually passing out.

With all crosshairs still aiming towards my hometown of Abbotsford, Cheyenne gets me to the Kamloops airport the next morning, where I board a last-minute flight. I think there's a layover in Alberta before heading back south. I have no clue if I'm hallucinating this entire travel. Messy splotches of memory explode and re-explode. A stewardess pours me a large glass of white wine. The clothes I've slept in for days feel damp, like parasites rubbing my body raw, generating heat to stay alive.

I fall asleep with my head in my lap, finally able to achieve that one impossible yoga pose I've been working towards my whole life.

When everything reappears in less of a blur, I awake in the back of a Taxi riding the rain-ridden roads toward Abbotsford.

Determined to kill all that's quarantined me from living a quality life in the last ten months for reasons still unknown to those who are able to do it, I miraculously find the off button to this out-of-control theme park ride. I'm able to fully wrench the taps closed with all I have left. Every speck of blood shared with the outside world; each tear, wince, scream, punch, thrust, breakdown, and emotion that was spent returned on the day of my last drink. Three more months of this will pass when I come to my senses at an old friend's house. I've just helped my friend Jessica (not my Ex from Chicago) move across town and have been bunking with her in the longest bender of my entire life, lasting a whole 30 days. Each day and night, 14 to 20 strong coolers are consumed. Strangely enough, I don't get too deathly ill during these final times. I believe a lot has to do with using psilocybin mushrooms from time to time as a way to begin a transformative escape away from Alcohol. The more scientific literature that is unearthed on the beatific wonders of mushrooms aiding in alcohol dependency is becoming brighter every single day.

With the undying and compassionate care from my friend Jessica, who also spent this entire time bringing her Indigenous holistic and spiritual methods to life, setting healing intentions around my body, my comfort levels skyrocketed, and eventually, we were able to guide me into the aura of recovery. I had begun to slowly taper off of the Alcohol (as I've done before) while also checking into an outpatient clinic to assess my health. From here, they prescribed me Gabapentin to fully ween off of the Alcohol, which helps to prevent complications from withdrawal. While it still felt like mere penniless scraps compared to Valium or Ativan, the Gabapentin does its work (still with horrible shakes and insomnia), and from this day forward, I have not touched a drop of Alcohol. My sober date is **June 5th, 2023**. I try not to let dates define who I am, but this will forever be mentally tattooed.

CHAPTER 19

Closure : To the Introvert using Alcohol to Socially Cope

Repairing the ladder that travels up from a fathomless Well takes patience and laser-like precision—the horrors of its bottomless macabre midnight stained water need to be remembered, not forgotten. To try to commit execution to memories of the past is to grant victory to the vile subduer of your crowned tyrannical King, lashing about, frothing at the mouth while committing genocide to all of the cells within you. It takes the most unrelenting heroes and heroines to confront one's own history head-on rather than stealthily tiptoeing around its parameters with a bottle in hand.

By the time this book comes out, I will be close to 600 days sober from Alcohol. There isn't and will never be a day that passes where I'm not plagued with reminiscing about the quality effects of what drinking booze promised me. I began witnessing it come alive through some of my first visually stored memories as a child. It persistently operated within my family circle, always lingering within my cold grasp. There is no doubt I was predestined to at least run into some sort of trouble with it due to the nature of my childhood environment.

While I could have made these entries and experiences all about seeking out blame and hostility towards others, trying to find irrefutable evidence that they may have been the whole reason behind this binge with the Devil; my current sober record due to holding myself accountable for my actions should speak volumes. The more my finger drunkenly wagged in the hateful winds of accusation & blame, the longer I would remain in inebriated, unrecoverable states of vicious, homicidal & emotionally suicidal patterns.

Wishing for nutritious crops that have already been cooked by the embers from the sky will go absolutely nowhere. Once the course of nature has taken its toll on an event in your life, there is no reason to keep revisiting it in a hopefully morose game of reprisal as you aimlessly wander off of a cliff. What's done is done, and that's all there is to it. Re-analyzing artifacts already dusted clean of the bone material of your life's antiquity provides no more restitution. Constantly swiping the victim card will be your passport toward a lifetime of zero hope of ever claiming the highest forms of recovery. Don't be the cracked record, mulling around with alcohol-ridden breath, replaying what you've wanted to say or do for the last three, five, ten or twenty years when you can shatter that fucking bottle to dust TODAY and craft a blooming horizon as opposed to rows of charred remains.

Evidently, if you are too far into the dependency stage, then it is absolutely necessary to seek medical intervention or begin to wean yourself off properly. Cold Turkeying off of Alcohol, now that you've read how seriously life-threatening and dangerous it can be, is one of the most foolish things you could ever do to yourself. Do it carefully and correctly, and you'll be granted another access pass to restart where you left off.

Sometimes, there is a lack of words, no matter what language you speak, to describe the complete and utter mentally disfiguring rape of the soul Delirium Tremens brings to an individual. Multiple times a week, I'm brought back to similar feelings of disarray, reminding me of swimming through the resharpened scythes of where I transcended when undergoing the DTs. Something as simple as remembering a previous event in my teenage years will invoke feelings of intense questioning. A specific conglomeration of colours. A study session after reading. A splotch on the wall. The patterns inside of a television signal. Sometimes, it's beautiful. Sometimes, it is pummeling. Either or, the DTs are a near-death experience. Like an intense hallucinogenic journey or other brushes with our final moments, these experiences reshape the way we forever perceive what's ahead of us.

Self-care is paramount to shuffling a promising deck toward the hand that takes home the largest jackpot. When you wander off and become bogged down with the chore of chiselling your physical statue away to appease the lives of others, the grip on sanity lessens, and your travels will only get worse from here on out.

While some may view it as blatantly selfish, I view it as the safest possible way to embrace sobriety and continue to play by its rules without causing a mass power outage. I'm speaking directly to those more on the side of introversion; it remains best if you come first before anybody or anything—only you. Even if you find yourself having to back out of social gatherings, group settings, or life events; alone time is required for some. Only when you've locked in enough time away from the bottle (and feel comfortable enough) will you be able to rework time away from yourself and into the field to play with others.

Some Alcoholics (like myself) may have been using booze to shape their life outside of closed doors into a presentable social creature in order to co-exist without the swinging chandeliers of anxiety upheaving them every chance they've had once in a group of more than one person. Simple wishes like asking for an unsocial (not anti-social) future are looked down upon by others as madness. There is a fiercely substantial difference between being a loner and the request to be left alone.

I spent the majority of my life being decimated by forcing myself into extroverted, imploding arenas collapsing in on me. It wasn't until I summoned the bravery to completely and totally put my interests at the front of the line that sobriety finally found me with legitimate, open arms. Eventually, it pulled me to the stadium's entrance to allow the orange sky glow to hand me the necessary tools to scale away from allowing others to make decisions for myself. All of us fear change. There is no chance in hell of ever becoming sober if you don't take down the *no trespassing signs* and open the front gate to allow it on your property.

Once you've learned to allocate the proper time to be spent inward rather than outward, doing so without the need for chemical interference masking your genuine identity, you will walk without such a dizzying gait toward reformatting and repairing each microfibre of life sacrificed for a round of drinks. Mentally, financially, physically, and spiritually; your life will usher these in via homeostasis. It won't be immediate, and the awkwardness of spending time by yourself will take some time to get used to, but like an incoming snowfall that plasters the sky with a cottony deep hue of purple and gray, the accommodation of solitude and silence is a beautiful thing.

The bottom line is... TAKE CARE OF YOUR SOBRIETY FIRST. You have to cease and desist everything you've ever done once engaged in the art of drinking. That means specific *friends* need to be let go of, social hangouts entirely avoided, and typical trigger patterns hung up by their throats for you to watch perish. While triggers aren't an immediate source of relapsing, they'll eventually make their way into your life when you least expect it and derail you beyond comprehension.

Chances are you grabbed this book either from knowing me personally, through the grapevine, or you want to take a glimpse through hollow eye sockets on where Alcoholism will eventually bring you or someone you know closely. Maybe you've been planning to stop for a while and have found yourself in a distorted web of trying to quit and trying to balance it at the same time.

That never works until it's too late. Not only will you start to lose those around you, but you'll painfully lose <u>crucial time</u> that's no longer able to be pulled back in your life. Like dropping your phone in an endless lake and diving after it with your eyes closed; the hopeless misery that follows is staggering.

Of course, each of us is splattered on the canvas with very different colourful results. I can only relay what has worked for me. Some are trapped in family trauma and relationships that just can't be so easily pushed to the side to begin a journey of self-retrospection. I hope for those suffering to get the chance to do so and watch their piles of worms grow into heaps of jewels.

Along with the loss of friendships, partners that could have very well been linked with me in marriage, and opportunities to pursue ventures that may have catapulted me to better outcomes (or to my death), the majority of the mental & physical scars I acquired along the way are held close as if a monumental exhibition. The tissue surrounding them is layered with jarring photographic memories, playing melodies written in such wretched states but bringing forth beauty and cues to look back and correct the night's trajectory before plunging into the rancid depths of binge drinking.

With as much might as I can muster, where some days the invitation back to the world of drinking seems impossible to ignore, I'm brought back to the reality of it all, looking down and surveying a body littered with the scars of surviving being trapped under an out-of-control wreck for years—the scars that maintain a vision that's propelled forward—the Scars for Future Wars.

About the Author

Jordan Jongema is a Multi-instrumentalist with 20+ years of performing, writing, and recording music. This is his first book. Jordan resides in the Southern Okanagan, in the city of Penticton, British Columbia, Canada.